The Fairy Kingdom

By
Geoffrey Hodson

THE BOOK TREE
San Diego, California

First published 1927
Theosophical Publishing House
London

ISBN 1-58509-212-6

Cover layout & design
Lee Berube

Printed on Acid-Free Paper
in the United States of America

Published by
The Book Tree
P O Box 16476
San Diego, CA 92176
www.thebooktree.com
We provide fascinating and educational products to help awaken the public to new ideas and
information that would not be available otherwise.
Call 1 (800) 700-8733 for our *FREE BOOK TREE CATALOG*.

INTRODUCTION

Are fairies real? What about gnomes, brownies, devas, angels, fauns, mannikins and nature spirits? Geoffrey Hodson explores the reality of all these beings (and more) in this entertaining and informative book.

The author has developed his own clairvoyant sense to such a degree that he can see and, in some cases, communicate with conscious entities that share our world. For those of us who have never seen any of these beings, Hodson does a great job in describing them. For example mannikins are small green creatures about 4 to 6 inches high with pointed ears and children's faces who seem to have a close relationship to grass and the trunks of trees. They are sometimes a bit taller, brown instead of green, and often do things that defy the laws of gravity. Brownies are little fat men about a foot tall who wear brown clothes, pointed caps and large brass buckles on their belts.

Many fascinating stories are found within this book, describing his encounters with these beings. Where does one look to find these creatures? Hodson knows all their favorite haunts and because of this has many adventures and observations to share.

He has seen nature spirits hovering between the tops of pine trees, fairies who hover over clover blossoms, and a large deva, or angel, that hovered motionless over 2000 feet above ground. A deva once informed the author that the Kingdom of Pan, of which all these creatures are members, is slowly passing away. What remains today is an old remnant of a previous epoch. Hodson also describes satyrs and fauns as being the last remnants of a more deeply involved stream of consciousness, one that gives them their weird and unusual vibration.

This is highly interesting when one considers the theories of Jacques Vallee, a modern UFO researcher. Vallee reveals that fairies, elves, gnomes and the like were more common in the past, but as humans modernized, this hidden consciousness has begun to appear in the form of a new mythology—one that better reflects our new, technological mindset. This makes sense when considering the UFOs we now see hovering motionless these days, instead of the older fairies and nature spirits as Hodson describes.

Fairies have disappeared in front of him, as UFOs have often done, and he states that the average height fairies rise in the air is about 15 to 20 feet. He conjectures that they rise to about 80 to 100 feet in order to travel.

In our modern world hundreds or possibly thousands of people claim to have been abducted by small alien creatures. Believe it or not, there were once hundreds of similar stories replete in local folklore, but the abductors were small elves instead of modern "aliens." Hodson did not make these connections because he wrote this book in the 1920's, years before the age of UFOs began and before they became widely noticed. But the parallels are strikingly similar and, at times, amazing.

To what extent is the reality of the beings in this book? At first, it is easy for us to dismiss them as nothing more than imaginative tales meant to fascinate and tantalize children. Yet upon reading this book, one comes away with interesting questions not previously considered. What Hodson makes clear is that we're dealing with a form of consciousness that is so alien to us that it is far easier to dismiss it than investigate it. Unless of course we begin to see it, like Hodson has. Once we begin to realize that entirely different yet valid forms of consciousness are out there, permeating nature beyond the visual spectrum that our eyes are able to see, then we are well on our way to accepting the reality of the Fairy Kingdom.

Paul Tice

THE KINGDOM OF GOD

In No Strange Land

O WORLD invisible, we view thee,
O World intangible, we touch thee,
O World unknowable, we know thee,
Inapprehensible, we clutch thee !

Does the fish soar to find the ocean,
The eagle plunge to find the air—
That we ask of the stars in motion
If they have rumour of thee there ?

Not where the wheeling systems darken,
And our benumbed conceiving soars !
The drift of pinions, would we harken,
Beats at our own clay-shuttered doors.

The angels keep their ancient places ;—
Turn but a stone, and start a wing !
'Tis ye, 'tis your estranged faces,
That miss the many-splendoured thing.

But (when so sad, thou couldst not sadder)
Cry ;—and upon thy so sore loss
Shall shine the traffic of Jacob's ladder
Pitched betwixt Heaven and Charing Cross.

Yea, in the night, my soul, my daughter,
Cry,—clinging Heaven by the hems ;
And lo, Christ walking on the water
Not of Gennesareth, but Thames !

Francis Thompson.

Acknowledgment

My thanks are due to the editor of the *Herald of the Star* for permission to reprint the sections in Chapter VIII. headed, Our Blessed Lady and Human Motherhood, Christmas at Huizen, 1925, Dr. Besant at the Queen's Hall, "Hark the Herald Angels Sing," Armistice Day, 1923, An Angel Friend at a Concert.

Preface

THE reception accorded to the book *Fairies at Work and at Play* encourages me to publish some notes of my further clairvoyant studies of the kingdom of Faery. I hope that this second book may help the reader to a closer understanding of the deva kingdom than did the first, in writing which both the subject and the method of research were entirely new to me. My object in making these later studies has been rather to contact the consciousness of angel and fairy than to describe and catalogue their forms.

To those to whom the idea of clairvoyance, as a means of research, is new, I would say that Theosophy teaches * that this sixth sense is latent in every man, and will one day be used as a natural means of cognition ; also, that it is possible, by self-training, to arouse it from latency to active expression, and to use it as a means of investigation.

The methods of training taught by Theosophy have nothing in common with those of mediumship and trance ; they aim at the conscious employment of the faculty, after it has been developed by means of expansion of consciousness attained by meditation, and the sensitising of the vehicles of consciousness in order that they may express the results of such expansion.

* *Vide Clairvoyance*, by C. W. Leadbeater ; *Man, Visible and Invisible*, by A. Besant and C. W. Leadbeater ; *Introduction to Yoga*, by A. Besant.

My studies have led me to regard the devas as potential co-workers with man in the fulfilment of the plan of God, and I look forward to a time when every institution, religious or secular, and every home, may be centres where co-operation between the two kingdoms prevails, the result of which will be a widening of the ideal of brotherhood to include devas and nature spirits in a truly universal Brotherhood of angels and of men.

GEOFFREY HODSON.

Contents

THE KINGDOM OF FAERIE

CHAPTER I

DEVAS

Genius Loci

Twice hath it come, that Presence !—once i' the grove
That skirts the russet fallow on yonder hill—
And now again, down by the little rill
At sunset. Aye, if thrill of heart may prove,
Twice in these fields, I have felt a Spirit move
That was not of the earth ! Silent it came,
A living ecstasy without a name,
And seemed to turn the very air to Love.
And yet, O whence ? Deep woodlands I have seen
That were as rich, yet lacked that rarer spell ;
Lanes as thick-flowered I know, and slopes as green.
Some God it is, some Genius of the place
Doth haunt, methinks, this spot, and loves it well,
And breathes his love in that diffused grace.

E. A. Wodehouse.

The Deva of a Cotswold Valley

August 4th, 1925.

THIS valley, which is about two miles long and one mile across, is in the charge of a nature-deva,* who seems to have come here in order to help forward the

---

* The word " deva " means " shining one," and is the Indian name for angel ; " deva " and " angel " are used throughout as referring to the same order of beings.

1

evolution of the life of the valley. Though he himself is a nature-spirit and would, therefore, be primarily interested in the evolving elemental and vegetable kingdoms, he also takes a close interest in the human inhabitants of the valley, and works for them when he can.

It is the evening of the day following our arrival, and we have climbed the hills, which rise out of the valley at its closed end, to a point from which we can look down upon the fields, houses and woods of which it is composed. As we are sitting gazing on the peaceful and beautiful scene the deva shows himself ; hovering in the air over the tree tops before us, he bids us welcome to the valley.

When first seen he appeared to be about ten feet high, and his aura radiated from his form to a distance of about 100 yards on all sides. After our conversation, however, he extended or stretched it, until it reached right across the valley, as well as down to the little stream which runs through it ; he then moved slowly down the valley, touching every living thing within it, giving to each a share of his own magnificently vital life force. His face is noble and beautiful, his eyes are dazzlingly bright, and look more like two centres of force than eyes, for they are not used to the same extent as ours, for the expression of thought and emotion. A benevolent welcome is expressed, not only through the smile which parts his lips, but in his whole bearing ; he radiates his welcome upon us, just as he sheds his purificatory and quickening power on the whole valley. The colours of his aura are brilliant and constantly changing, as they flow in waves and vortices outwards from the central form. The colour scheme changes minute by minute ; now the predominating colour may be a deep royal blue with red and golden yellow and green sweeping across and through it, making eddies and waves of brilliant colour as they flow outwards in a continuous stream ; now they change completely—there is a background of pale rose-du-Barry, with a soft eau-de-nil, sky blue and the palest of yellows. Occasionally, where the mighty auric pinions are outlined in golden fire, he looks like a great bird with the edges of its wings lit up by the setting sun. There is a continual play of force, like a miniature Aurora Borealis, rising from his head, high up into the air, and in the middle of the head there is a blazing centre of light, which is the seat of the consciousness in the form. As I describe him, he has suddenly risen into the heavens, where he hovers so high up as to be almost invisible. Even at this height, however, he still holds the valley within his consciousness.

His character is an unusual combination of the deva's vivid sense of freedom from all limitations and the human capacity for tenderness, deep concern for others, and love. I feel sure that every birth and death within the valley must be known to him, and that the pain, which accompanies both, is eased by him to the utmost of his power ; for I see memory-forms in his aura, which show him taking within its glowing radiance the souls of those, who have but just died, sheltering them, and guiding them to a place of peace ; I see that he watches the children at play, and the old folk taking their ease ; he is, indeed, the guardian angel of the valley, and happy are they who live within his care.

The hosts of lesser nature spirits obey him, and I see

the earth-men and the tree-men and the lower fairies
answering to his touch as his power rushes out upon
them; the elves and the brownies feel a sudden
exaltation, the source of which they cannot fully
comprehend, though they recognise it to be a constant
feature of their lives; the fairies feel an added frolic-
someness and joy as he plays upon them with his
radiant life. All Nature seems to be quickened by his
presence here.

His influence gives a certain quality, a local characteristic, a special atmosphere, distinctly noticeable
throughout the whole length of the valley, which has a
charm amounting almost to glamour; it must also
affect every human being who lives here for any length
of time, particularly those who are born and live
within the continual play of his auric life, and there
surely must be times when they feel the spirit of the
deva upon them.

A DEVA CEREMONY

The Hotel Balcony, Grand Salève, Switzerland.
Evening, June 4th, 1925.

The Mont Blanc group is evidently an occult centre.
Very great forces are visible playing in and around the
massif this evening. They appear like tongues of flame
coming out of the body of the mountain, passing up the
side and shooting high into the air. Upon the central
peak (Mont Blanc itself) a continual stream of energy,
like an intensified radio-activity, is visible; brilliant
lights flash and dart through it, as the devas fly backwards and forwards in the midst of this display of
dynamic energy.

There is an occult ceremony taking place on and around the summit, and it appears that it has evoked the power and presence of the deva hosts. In the centre is a group of great angels, all of whom are armed with swords ; their movements are relatively slow, and of a definite and orderly character, and they appear to be passing through some recognised evolutions. At intervals streams of energy rush out into the upper air like gigantic sky-rockets, while all around, on the edge of the central group, are numbers of mountain-devas, wild and fierce. I feel that these must be the beings from whom Wagner drew the musical inspiration for the Valkyries (the opera, *Die Walküre*, was written within a mile of this place), for I recognise a close resemblance between them and his Valkyries, as also between their vibration and that of the opera. They swoop down over the snowfields and glaciers to the lower levels, passing down the sides of the mountains at great speed ; the call of the Valkyries is easily recognisable.

As I dictate, the intensity of the activity on the summit increases, and the mountain begins to resemble a volcano in eruption, without the smoke. I find my consciousness being drawn far out into space beyond the confines of this planet, and feel that phenomena, similar to that described, are occurring at other points of the solar system. Force begins to flash to and fro between these points, and power to descend on to the earth. The " Valkyries " are becoming wilder and wilder in their activities, as if driven mad by the fiery energy of the display ; they are absorbing it, carrying it to distant places and discharging it into the earth. I become conscious of rings upon rings, hierarchy upon hierarchy of the devic hosts, groups of mighty beings bathed in dazzling white light.

Now sound is added to sight ; I hear music, solemn and majestic, as of the great Gandharvas * themselves ; it is like the music of heavenly choirs, hymning far out in space, chanting great cosmic symphonies.

As far as the earth is concerned, the whole pheno-menon seems to be centred upon Mont Blanc ; even the rings of devas seem to rise, circle upon circle, vertically above the peak. Up the channel so formed rushes the power from the earth, and down it also streams the response—looking like a pillar of fire whose base rests upon the *massif*—bathing the whole moun-tain and surrounding district in glorious light. The force descends deep down into the earth, and must surely be connected with the spirit thereof ; it seems as if the spirits of the planets were communing through the medium of the devic hierarchy.

The force appears to exist as high up as the causal plane and probably beyond, while it also is producing prodigious effects at the astral level. The astral vibrations resulting are clearly noticeable at this dis-tance (*i.e.*, thirty miles away) ; they come like tidal waves, which go sweeping past, and are lost in the distance. I can see them, still rushing forward far down the valley of the Rhône. At the mental level the effect is more far-reaching, though it seems, by contrast, to be less powerful and more concentrated at the centre. The downpouring stream no longer appears solid, but resembles liquid fire, white and silvery blue.

By now the stream has widened considerably, and

* *Gandharva* is the Indian name for the angels of music.

must include the whole of the Mont Blanc group. Count-less numbers of devas surround it in serried ranks, and there is also a constant passing to and fro, arrival and departure ; everything living, including the mountain itself, is marvellously vivified, while many of the devas seem literally intoxicated. Sharing the consciousness of one as he passes, I find myself thrilled with a sense of boundless energy, of resistless power, which I must bear away swiftly through space to my appointed station on some other part of the planet.

*   *   *   *   *

Now at last the ceremony seems to be drawing to a close, the number of the attendant devas decreases ; they disperse, travelling swiftly in their various directions, each one glowing with the power he has received, till at last only the central officiants themselves remain ; the general feeling of electric hyperactivity begins to fade, though the actual brilliance of the light upon the summit is undiminished.

If one may draw conclusions from a single experience of this kind, they would be that the devas use ceremonial as a means of evoking and distributing power, and that they play an important part in interplanetary communication.

CHAPTER II

NATURE-SPIRITS OF WIND AND BLOSSOM

Coneyhurst Hill, Hurtwood, near Ewhurst.
April 17th, 1926.

WE are sitting at the edge of a wood consisting of the very old larch and pine trees which cover this sandstone hill; from the southern slopes we are able to see a wide panorama of beautiful countryside, which stretches away to the South Downs.

An atmosphere of spontaneous joyousness and gaiety pervades all the activities of the various members of the deva evolution, who are to be found in this neighbourhood.

There is a strong south-westerly wind, in which sylphs are to be seen disporting themselves; their gambols consist of long, swift, straight rides down the wind for miles and miles until they are lost in the distance; or of twists, turns and sudden upward dartings, followed by breathless dives, which cease abruptly just above the treetops, and are again followed by an equally swift ascent thousands of feet into the air. Here and there, groups combine in a wild aerial dance, with their auras streaming out behind them as if blown by the wind, their eyes wild with excitement; intoxicated

8

with joy, they swing in great circles, suddenly formed, and as suddenly broken, exulting in the power and vital energy with which their aerial home is charged on this wonderful morning of spring.

Under these conditions they frequently lose all semblance of human form, seeming to become whirling masses of force and vital energy, in which suddenly appear graceful wing-like formations, long streaming curves, a suggestion of waving arms, and of hair flying in the wind; ever and anon two blazing eyes appear, and a face of unearthly beauty, combining in its expression in a way utterly impossible to human kind, exaltation, intoxicating ecstasy, and a fierce virility and power. Just now one paused, hovering so near that he appeared to fill the heavens with his brilliant aura and to dominate the whole field of vision with his dynamic presence; in a flash he was gone, disappearing in the remote distance, covering leagues and leagues of the " wide savannahs of the blue " in a second of time; he seemed driven by an energy and charged with a power over which he himself had but partial control, as if he had drunk so deeply of aerial vitality—of the power of the wind which sweeps down the Weald, setting the firs a-sighing with that long, sweeping song of their kind, which is so strangely like the distant roar of the sea—that he was unable to maintain a stationary position.

Contact with the consciousness of the sylph in this condition suggests to me a state of concentrated energy similar to that found within the atom; it produces the feeling of compression, almost to bursting point, of incalculable energy, awe-inspiring in its potency, yet harmless because confined to prescribed channels of flow. I am almost oppressed by the contrast between this vivid existence and our human life in the flesh, which appears to be so dull and limited within these heavy, unresponsive human forms. Even at the mental level I, for one, would stand no chance in a race with a sylph, for whilst I was making up my mind to start, he would have reached the winning-post. The very matter of his body is alive and instinct with energy and motion ; it would seem that, whilst to us will-power must be exerted in order to move, with such an one as him, who has just filled and flooded the atmosphere about us with his vivid presence, the opposite is true, for it seemed almost impossible for him to remain still.

Yet even while I attempt this description, I am forced to the conclusion, that this statement must be confined to certain members of the sylph family, by the splendid vision of a deva hovering, relatively motionless, some 2,000 feet above the ground. Fifteen to twenty feet high, he is bathed in a shimmering white opalescence, which seems to play continually through and over him. Studying this phenomenon more closely, the force, of which it is an expression, appears to arise within the central form—human, and as if robed in this white radiance—along its whole length and continually to flow outwards in waves to the edge of the aura. The predominating colour continually changes, like that of an opal which is flashed in the sun, though infinitely more delicate ; now blue, now rose, now soft apple-green, sweep through and suffuse the whole aura, though the noble head and face remain a delicate rose. The arms are slightly extended from the sides ; in this pose, with the power playing from him in all directions

and reaching to distances varying from ten to twenty
yards from the central form, this great deva " stands "
high up in the heavens. He appears once to have
belonged to the order of sylphs and to have evolved
beyond their race. Around, above and below him his
younger brethren play, making his poise the more
marked by contrast with their swift mobility, their
rapid travelling through space.

Once more the hierarchical order is revealed, for he
seems to be an advanced deva, in some way responsible
for the lives and evolutionary progress of his brethren.
In spite of the intense concentration of the higher levels
of his consciousness, he has become aware of my
endeavour to contact him, and his answering recognition has flooded me with such measure of his power as
I am able to receive. The effect is interesting to
observe ; my mental and astral bodies—temporarily
illuminated—tend to arrange themselves in a formation
somewhat resembling that of his own ; his force
" descends " from the causal levels and wells up from
within my mental and astral bodies, charging them with
power and then flowing off to the edge ; even down in
the dense physical a strong vibration plays.

The deva is the centre of considerable activity among
the sylphs, numbers of whom are continually approaching him ; it appears that some form of communication
takes place between him and them, after which they
depart to their several spheres of activity. Some of
them are nature-devas and are concerned with the
vegetable kindgom. Though his consciousness is
active at the lower mental levels, his form is visible at
the astral, and most of those who approach him do so
there. They are brilliantly coloured wood and tree

devas, many of whom show in their auras the form and
colour of the tree or wood with which they are concerned;
some of them are evidently connected with fruit trees
now in blossom, and their auras show forth the colours
of the fruit orchard or tree in full bloom. Evidently
the association of a nature-spirit with a tree has the
effect of impressing the form of the tree upon its aura,
either by a system of repercussion or through the
strong mental self-identification of the nature-spirit
with the tree ; in this way they seem to carry their
work with them to their chief, who is able to observe
it by this means, and to correct, as well as to influence
it directly.

The reader may have some difficulty in conceiving
of a deva, whose aura contains the form and colour of,
say, an apple tree in blossom. Following one of these
nature-spirits back to its work, I see that it " settles "
into the tree, which it allows its aura completely to
enfold. Apparently it remains in this position for
considerable periods of time, influencing the development of the vegetable consciousness, as well as of the
lesser nature-spirits, by the continual play of its own
more vivid life forces. As a result of this method of
work, the continued play of the life force of the tree—
along the fixed lines of trunk, branch, stem, leaf and
blossom—impresses itself upon the aura. The effect
is most beautiful, as a number of such nature-spirits
rise together from an orchard, taking duplicates of
their charges up into the air with them ; as they hover,
still keeping more or less together, each rising and
falling a little, waves are formed of these replicas of
snowy white blossom ; then, as if at a signal, the whole
company spreads out and rises into the aura of the deva,

taking with it the atmosphere of beauty, joy, and the spring-like freshness of newly-awakened Nature. He appears to scrutinise and then to bless ; sometimes he enfolds an individual or group more closely in his aura and holds it there, releasing it later. They look like a flight of wonderful birds as they return to their respective duties.

In some way this affects him, and his aura increases in size and brilliancy as his work proceeds. Streams of light proceed from him down to the ground, as his blessing is borne through the air by his charges, and the whole phenomenon of their " morning's work " begins to assume proportions beyond the power of my feeble pen to describe, as also of my mind to comprehend.

At the risk of materialising the whole conception, I might liken it to an enormous business concern, the head of which controls and guides its activities through his many agents, he himself remaining within the privacy of his office. Unlike modern business, however, the whole of this vast field of work is pervaded by an atmosphere of exceeding great joy, of complete natural co-operation and implicit acceptance of the leader and obedience to his behests.

From the top of this hill we look down upon the Weald of Surrey and Sussex, which stretches westwards, southwards and eastwards into what is called " the garden of England." The experience I have been describing has made me realise the appropriateness of the term, and has also given me a wider appreciation of the work of the deva hierarchy in the fulfilment of the plan of the Great Gardener of the Universe.

CHAPTER III

Letchworth.   January 3rd, 1925.

FOR the last six months, I have been aware that a
member of the gnome family, who has succeeded in
obtaining a greater measure of self-consciousness than
some of his brethren, has been taking an increasing
interest in us.   In the summer-time he would generally
appear as we entered the garden from the house, running out from the orchard across the lawn, and attract-
ing my attention by etheric flashes.   Very little notice
was taken of him at that time, but since the coming of
winter he has begun to enter the house.   During our
evenings around the fire, he is frequently to be seen
playing about the room, passing in and out of the
windows, and showing quite as much interest in us as
would, say, a tamed bird or squirrel.

He is exactly one foot eight inches in height.   I have
been able to measure him because his head reaches the
tip of a certain ornamentation on the legs of the piano.
His skin is very dark, and his body of a spongy texture,
rather like soil, which has been frozen and has thawed.
In the garden he used to run about without any clothing, although occasionally he would colour his body a
dull green.   I notice this evening, however, that he has
made a definite attempt at a suit, but, curiously enough,

14

the effect is not produced by the addition of a materialised garment, but by a change in the actual surface
of his body, except in the case of his imitation white
collar. This, obviously, is an addition ; moreover, it
is one to which he appears to attach considerable
importance, for when it fades, as it continually does,
he remakes it as soon as he notices its absence ; in fact,
he does not allow it to fade out completely, and its
continual re-materialisation occupies a good deal of
his time just now. The lines and edges of his coat and
waistcoat, the latter complete with buttons, appear in
the texture of what corresponds to his skin, and he
obtains a considerable measure of permanency in the
markings. With trousers he has not yet achieved
much success, and as far as I can observe he has made
no attempt at any kind of footwear. His neck and
arms are thin, and too long for our sense of proportion,
and his head and limbs appear so loose and spongy that
he reminds me of a rag doll in that respect ; yet he can
stiffen them to a certain extent at will, as he has been
doing in the performance of the sort of shambling
dance, by means of which he gave expression to his
feelings of pleasure at our return from a ten days'
absence. The movements of this dance consisted of
swaying the body from side to side, the legs being kept
together and being allowed to bend outwards, first to
the right and then to the left, the arms being raised
above the head at the same time. These movements
did not entail a change of position in the room, although
some sort of slow circular drift resulted.

The face is most unprepossessing, being nearly black,
and the forehead is long and very sloping. There are
no eyebrows, very little eye-socket, two beady black

eyes like shoe buttons, thin, rather sunken cheeks, long pointed nose, wide mouth, by the aid of which, together with the expression of his eyes, he is able to register something in the nature of a smile of pleasure. The chin is small and not fixed in shape, but varying according to the expression of his face. The arms finish in the appearance of a closed fist ; his feet are about eight inches long, and pointed.

Unprepossessing and stupid as this description may make him appear, there is quite a bright little spirit inhabiting that body. Although he is not capable of anything approaching real affection, he finds sufficient pleasure in our society to make him forsake his usual haunts, for the unusual environment of the inside of a house. He is able to recognise my wife and myself as distinct from each other and from other people, and in our company he finds quite definite pleasure. He is not as sensitive to the vibrations of our astro-mental auras as are the other orders of nature-spirits, and can come quite close to our physical bodies, feeling only pleasure in those of our vibrations to which he can respond. After a time he feels a definite stimulation, and something passes through his little body which corresponds in the world of solids to a warm glow. When this reaches a certain point he partially de-materialises and floats out into the garden as if, in that subtler state, he gravitated towards his own world. As soon as the effect dies away, which it does in a few minutes, he returns and walks about the room quite unconcernedly.

Looking into his mind—by an extension of the faculties which enable me to see his form—I find no memory of this experience, nothing, in fact, beyond a vague sense, that it is pleasant to be here. There is an instinctive recognition that the contents of the room are familiar to him, but no definite memory of any previous contact with them. He does not see any object as we do. When on the ground he sees the legs of furniture and of people ; he has no understanding of any upper portion being connected with them. I am not able to see how he recognises us, although he certainly shows a preference for us, and in the summer often appeared immediately we stepped out of the house. As I dictate this he is standing just behind me, and in his mind there is no knowledge of my having any existence higher than my hips ; in fact, his conception of me just now, looks to me like an animated pair of trousers. That conception satisfies him fully. If, however, he sees me from a distance, he sees a little higher, say to the shoulders and above that a kind of shining mist. He both sees and feels the health aura, and likes to stand within it and to receive an etheric shower-bath.

March 20th, 1925.

After a passage of three months an opportunity occurred for further study of the gnome. He had frequently been seen in the house and garden, but, apart from a greeting and a glance in his direction, no special attention had been paid to him. Investigating his circumstances more closely, I find that he has been made the subject of a special experiment by a deva, who seems to occupy the position of guardian over the elemental life in the garden and the large orchard surrounding it, where many thousands of young fruit trees are growing. This deva is evidently much concerned with the task of quickening the evolution of his charges, and his attitude is very like that of an animal breeder or of a gardener, who might select this or that animal or plant for special treatment. He observed that the gnome had become friendly with us, and decided to take advantage of the fact.

One result of this appears to be a considerable increase of the natural imitative tendency of the gnome. He now wears a white collar, which bids fair to become permanent, and a dark coat, and his lower limbs are losing their lanky thinness and are beginning to resemble the legs of trousers. Again, I notice that these changes are not produced in the usual fairy way, as additional clothing, but are actual modifications of the etheric body of the gnome. Most remarkable of all is the change in his face, which is becoming distinctly lighter in colour and rounder in shape. At first I thought that an entirely new nature-spirit had entered the room, but it is indeed the same little friend, for the gnome nature and form are easily detected " under the skin." His intelligence is distinctly brighter, and his self-assurance greatly increased, for he has climbed on to my knee, though not without some misgivings, judging by the expression of his face. I now see that he did not do this of his own volition, but under a strong suggestion, almost hypnotic, of the deva who is watching. I was barely conscious, physically, at the time when he climbed on to my knee, as I was trying to contact the mind of the deva ; I felt a tremor, a distinct coldness and a very slight weight on my knee, which attracted my attention—and there was the little man. He cannot see the deva, as he does not possess astral sight, but he recognises a familiar influence, and instinctively obeys the suggestions which accompany it.

It is evident that gnomes in their normal state are actuated almost entirely by group consciousness, and that all their activities, indeed, their whole lives, are expressions of instinctive impulses, which affect the whole tribe. Only when their attention is very much attracted to some external object, and the consciousness is drawn down into the etheric form, is there a semblance of self-consciousness, and even then it is very fleeting. Evolutionary progress for them is marked by a gradual increase in the power of external awareness, by the length of time during which they can maintain it, and by an increase in the degree of their self-consciousness.

Assisted by the deva, I see that a time eventually comes when the sense of self-consciousness becomes relatively permanent and the gnome will leave his tribe in complete forgetfulness and undertake work, or indulge in play, by himself. This accounts for, and explains, the fact mentioned in my first book on fairies, that gnomes were found as solitaries, as well as in groups. He says that it is possible to individualise, from the gnome stage, directly into the ranks of the sylphs, though this is not usual, an intermediate elemental kingdom generally being entered for a time. It is difficult to conceive of the swart and earthy gnome becoming a fairy, but the deva says it is not unusual, and that, as the time for change approaches, the gnomes take more and more interest in plants, flowers and trees, gradually lose their earthy character and their affinity with that element, and take on the characteristics of the fairy. I remember with interest, how puzzled I used to be at seeing gnomes connected with trees and having wings, but it appears—and the deva confirms it—that these were transition stages. He explains that, after passing through such metamorphoses, the gnome finds himself in one of the families of larger fairies, such as those connected with trees or the larger kinds of flowering plants ; rarely, if ever, does he start his new cycle of aerial evolution as one of the smaller flower fairies such as were photographed—he being distinctly superior to them in the evolutionary scale.

In the particular case we are studying, the idea seems to be to bring the gnome into as close and continuous contact with humanity as possible ; the deva adds : " Into an atmosphere where occult influences play." In other words, he is making use of the fact that we are students of Theosophy and of the link which every member of the Theosophical Society has with the occult hierarchy that governs the world. He says that the changes produced have occurred in about fourteen months, as he started the experiment at the beginning of last year. He also places the gnome in very frequent contact with the gardener here, and I see that the gnome follows him about and plays around him while he works. Though the whole affair has a distinctly humorous side, the deva takes it very seriously.

The deva himself is a very detached individual, and, though friendly, tends to regard me as a useful part of his experiment, and more as an accessory to it, than as a person ; from his point of view the whole of the fairy life of the garden and orchard is affected to a considerable degree by theosophical vibrations from the house ; it appears that our meditations and healing practices send forth influences into the garden, which help the evolution of the elemental kingdoms. This is why the deva is interested in us and tries to take as full advantage as possible of our presence here. He is benign, yet peculiarly aloof, being concerned almost exclusively with his work upon his own kingdom of Nature.

The whole of this estate of thirty-three acres is included in his sphere of influence, though not in his actual aura. His method reminds me of that employed by the deva of the wood at Nateby, described in *Fairies at Work and at Play*. He works chiefly from a central position in the air over the estate at a height from which he can conveniently keep the whole area within his influence. He has insulated it at the mental, astral and etheric levels by enclosing it in " walls " built by thought power. He employs two methods : one is to pour a general quickening influence from his own ego down into the whole estate, providing a condition for the fairies similar to that which a greenhouse provides for plants ; he is also in contact with higher sources of spiritual power, for which he is a channel to his younger brethren. The other method is by an expansion of his own aura, the forces of which he allows to play upon various parts of the garden and upon different groups of nature-spirits. He is extremely adept at this work, using his aura with the same ease with which we use our limbs ; he easily covers an acre of ground with it at a time, and increases its brilliance and density, affecting either the whole, or part of it, at will.

Though he is working at the levels of form his consciousness extends into the formless worlds, where he is to be seen as an ego of considerable advancement. He ranges through the three planes down to the etheric with great ease, maintaining at the same time his activity at the egoic level, and his contact with his equals and superiors. He uses his vehicles with such freedom, and is so obviously master of his work at each level, that it does not seem possible that the free flow of power and consciousness between ego and personality should ever be broken or even endangered ; in this he differs considerably from those of his human brethren, who, in their kingdom, are making corresponding endeavours. The tremendous impediment of possessing a physical body and of being partly imprisoned within it, becomes very obvious by comparison, and the exceedingly limiting and imprisoning effect of the dense physical body is realised almost painfully. In the deva's consciousness I see nothing which corresponds to pain, disappointment, depression, fear, anger or desire ; neither is there any sign of strain, or of that intense effort which is required by us to overcome the inertia of the lowest planes ; nor has he to resist those promptings of the lower nature with which the human aspirant to the spiritual life is assailed. The content of his mind appears to be, primarily, an intense intellectual interest in his work, which shows itself by the brilliant golden yellow, which is the predominant colour of his aura, affection for his charges showing as rose, sympathetic interest in their progress and extreme adaptability showing as apple green with flashes of emerald, the whole frequently irradiated by strong currents of a vivid and fiery white, which represents the ardour of his nature, stimulated and aroused by the higher forces for which he is a channel.

It is not easy to estimate his size, as it varies very much; when I first saw him this evening he had descended until he was partly in the room, and he then appeared to be about eight feet high, as far as his actual form was concerned; but at his station, to which he has now returned, having released the auric forces which were temporarily held in check, he looks much larger—perhaps twelve feet in height, while his aura spreads out to about twenty yards all round him at the astral and thirty to forty yards at the mental level; it is roughly ovoid in shape, though without a clearly defined edge, but he can extend it to three or four times its natural size, or cause the whole of its forces to be turned downwards and outwards so as to play upon the area under his charge. He seems to gravitate naturally to a point about 100 or 150 feet above the ground. I am inclined to think from this closer examination, that he is really interested in us, not to say attached, in his deva way; for there is a distinct feeling of brotherly recognition of us by him, and now that he is less concentrated on his experiment with the gnome (who, by the by, still remains playing about the room), his beautiful and noble face has softened into a smile; in response to my promise to help in his work, in my limited human way, he stretches forth his hand in blessing, and floods us for a moment with his vital energy.

CHAPTER IV

In the Cotswolds. A field of clover.
August 2nd,1925.

THERE is a kind of nature-spirit here, which belongs to the true fairy type, and appears to be intimately associated with the clover. It has a female form, usually of about three feet in height, but capable of enlargement to full human stature. This faculty of enlargement is being exercised to a greater degree than I have observed before, and is very frequently used between periods of " work." For the purpose of a more detailed description, I have selected a fairy who has approached us and hovers with her feet just above the heads of the clover blossom. The form is completely covered by a flowing auric garment ; there is an under or inner garment of soft green of a texture almost like chiffon, through which the faintest hint of a rose-coloured form is visible now and then, as changes occur in the direction and form of the flow of auric forces. Over this inner garment, and mingled with it, are bands of the colour of the clover flower, which, running through the aura, appear superimposed over the green ; they take no permanent form, though they suggest lines flowing downwards over the shoulders which come together at the waist and then widen out again as

24

they flow down the sides into the lower portions of
the aura.

Once more the faculty of imitation shows itself, for,
as I endeavour to obtain an exact description, the
particular fairy from whom it is taken has begun to
imitate the Austrian cloak which I am wearing, using
up the mauve clover colour to make the cloak. She is
quite fearless and friendly, and " stands " some five or
six yards away, thus enabling me to see clearly what
a beautiful creature she is. Forces flow through her
aura from a point corresponding to the solar plexus,
which seems to be the vital part of her " body " ; it is
golden yellow in colour, and glows like a miniature sun ;
its radiations look like fine golden lines streaming
throughout the whole aura ; they part on either side
of the neck and flow out to the edge of the aura, faintly
suggesting wings. There is another centre in the head,
of a silvery-white colour, from which, also, streams of
force are radiating—chiefly into the air over the head ;
this represents the astro-mental activity, and is constantly changing in colour and form.

The head is that of a young girl, hair and eyebrows
dark brown, face prettily rounded, colour fresh and
healthy-looking ; the hair is worn long, flows backwards and downwards from the forehead, and is lost
in a stream of auric force ; the shape of the limbs is
not visible through the green auric garment described
above, but the feet are encased in green tight-fitting
delicately modelled boots, the tops of which open out
like the petals of a flower above the ankles, which
appear to be encased in green stockings. The petals
are of a slightly darker shade of green, and there is a
touch of yellow about them somewhere, although its

position is not constant. The green robe previously referred to is very full and loose, and, being of extremely light texture, is in constant motion, as though continually played upon by a light wind. Occasionally the whole central form becomes clearly outlined. Her demeanour is light-hearted and playful. She holds both hands out before her, as if inviting us to join her in some fairy gambol amongst the clover.

She is now making gestures of great beauty which follow each other with exceeding swiftness. I can catch three of them. She begins by bringing the hands and arms together stretched downwards before her to their full length, palms touching, fingers extended. Both arms then make a circular movement outwards and upwards, pausing a moment level with the shoulders and meeting again fully extended over the head. Keeping the palms together, she brings the arms slowly down, stretched to their full extent before her to their first position, from which she repeats the process. She has now reversed this movement and has added two more radii by pausing for a fraction of a second at the positions midway between the horizontal and the vertical. The effect of this has been to stimulate the activity of the solar plexus centre to such a degree, that all appearance of the garment previously described disappears, as also does all semblance of human form below the shoulders, leaving only the solar plexus and head centres with their radiations of streaming force. She has vitalised herself by these gestures, which she is constantly repeating, and to which she is adding others so rapid that it is impossible to keep pace with her. She is now making radii with both arms—one arm stretched before her and one behind—thus forming "spokes" again at positions midway between the horizontal and the vertical ; but, while the radii of the first exercise described were those of a flat disc facing the spectator, these last add another dimension to the figure, and give the diameters for a complete sphere. It is interesting to note that the hands and fingers are kept fully extended and that lines of force stream out from them to a distance of about eight inches, adding considerably to the beauty of the effect. By this time she has worked herself up into a condition of exaltation ; she has constructed, by the movement of her arms and hands, a complete sphere around herself of about seven feet in height, in which there are two foci—one at the solar plexus and one at the head—holding the same position relatively to each other and the spherical form, as do the twin foci of an ellipse. The face and arms are still discernible, but all other suggestion of human appearance has gone ; there is simply a globe of outrushing force, the edge of which is quite clearly defined. Beyond this edge there is a pearly grey shimmer which, also, consists of radiating lines of force.

Contact with her consciousness, in its present condition, gives the feeling of most radiant happiness, of an intensity of pleasure quite beyond any normal human state. Unlike the water-spirits who, having reached the apex of exaltation, immediately discharge the force with which they are filled, she appears able to hold the condition. She is now withdrawing from the form she has made, rising slowly above it to a higher level of the astral plane, fading out of it, as it were, until the consciousness, leaving the shining globe floating motionless in the air, slips away and apparently returns

to the group-soul. The form still remains vivid, clear
and radiant.

In order to experiment, I directed a stream of force
into the sphere ; it penetrated and passed through it
without resistance, and without the form being dis-
turbed, and I received a feeling of the same stability
as that of the gyroscope. The form does not resist the
passage of force through it, but does resist any effort to
change its shape or position ; for example, I tried to
lift it into the air without success.

There are globes similar to this in different parts of
the field, and fairies, like the one described, with
variations in size, colour of hair and complexion.
Those that are actually working upon the clover sink
down into it, merging themselves in the astral double
of the crop, including within themselves an area of
about eighteen inches to two feet. They remain in this
state for a time, then spring up, hover awhile in the air,
fly to another part of the field, and repeat the process.
The field is about two acres in extent, and there must be
at least a hundred fairies working upon it.

One effect of their labours is to quicken the astral
consciousness of that part of the vegetable group-soul,
which is incarnated in this field. It seems evident,
that when a plant has reached the stage of flowering,
the ensouling consciousness is at its most active state ;
it is then very responsive to the stimulus provided by
the members of the deva hierarchy. One can almost
sense a kind of straining upwards of the plant consciousness towards the fairy, in that area in which it is
working, and there is certainly a quickening of the
evolutionary processes.

*   *   *   *   *

(*Ten minutes later.*) The fairy globe still persists. At present I do not see in the mind of the fairy any particular purpose in the formation of the globe; there is, of course, the natural creative joy in the production of an object of beauty. No doubt some use is made of these globes, though at the moment I cannot discover their purpose: perhaps they form reservoirs of force, which is gradually discharged into the vegetable group-soul.

A number of fairies are now dancing round the particular globe, which I have been describing, bathing in its radiant atmosphere and getting evident pleasure from the contemplation of its beauty. They have made a complete circle round it, and are passing through evolutions something like those of a country dance. These, in their turn, are producing a form; they are building a petal-shaped bowl, in which the sphere is resting, as they dance; the petals rise higher and higher, till they reach a level just above that of the top of the sphere, making a most beautiful flower-like form about eight to ten feet in diameter and eight feet high—a sort of model flower on the astral plane, a thing of glorious beauty and of perfect proportion. As I watch, the petals have grown higher still, and are gradually closing over the globe. The fairies' dancing and singing—I do not hear the sound, but judge by the movement of their mouths and expressions of their faces that they are singing—become wilder, as though a climax were approaching; they have risen above the ground and continue to encircle the form they have built, at the height of about three feet, their heads thrown back, their hair streaming down, the rosy sheen of their limbs appearing as they dance. Their pose and gestures are most beautiful.

During these evolutions, their eyes remain fixed intently upon the petals, for each of which there appears to be one fairy responsible. They are exercising a form-building power, in the use of which they appear to be adept ; an intense concentration is maintained by each one, the gaze being fixed at the highest point to which the petals have grown. Now the petals bend in a graceful curve towards the centre, where they gradually meet and join. The fairies have risen level with the top, still dancing and singing, still with their eyes upon their work ; they have made a complete flower form, not quite spherical, being narrower at the bottom than the top, where it is almost flat ; its shape is singularly beautiful, and the lines of the original petals, though all are now joined into one, are still visible. They have made an encasing shell of pure white iridescence, shot with green and clover colour ; through this glows faintly the globe which it encases.

The fairies break their circle at one point, open out into a line, move across the field to another globe, round which they start a similar process. This is going on in several parts of the field where the astral elemental essence is being moulded into forms like the first. Thus are born, and thus grow the " flowers " of the astral plane.

Grand Salève, near Geneva. June 5th, 1925.

There is a type of fairy here which does not seem to have the usual human form, but which, though it may be able to produce one, apparently does not do so, contenting itself with a face and head. At the same time the aura is much denser where the form would be, and the activity there is both greater than, and different from, that in the rest of the aura ; this shows as a continual series of colour changes, suggestive of a swiftly spinning wheel with slightly curved bands of colour from the centre to the circumference, crossing as they spin. Each band appears to have several different colours, and to have a motion of its own in addition to the general circular movement. The movement of the bands is somewhat like the opening and closing of scissors, and gives one the impression of continual streaming of colour inwards and outwards from the centre. All the colours of the spectrum are present in their softest shades, and many wonderful combinations are being produced all the time ; this activity is not only two-dimensional, but has an effect at least in the third.

A particular fairy that I am observing is a fascinating and charming creature ; moreover, she is by no means averse either to our company or to my scrutiny. The face resembles that of a very pretty young country girl, and is continually wreathed in smiles of the most engaging character. There are large numbers of these fairies on the hillsides, all very similar in appearance, though varying a little in expression and in the colour of the hair. The very dark-haired variety seems to be more serious, and some of them have quite an imperious expression. The complexion is white, with just a little colour.

Though they can rise high into the air, they remain for the most part just above the tips of the long grass, occasionally descending into a clump of wild flowers. When they do this, the fairy form disappears, and the aura spreads itself out to include the plant, or clump, as the case may be. In one sense they may be said to brood over their charges, yet they also inform them, so that they are doubly ensouled—first by their own natural evolving life, and secondly by the far more vivid consciousness of the fairy. While the aura is so expanded, certain rhythmic movements are noticeable in it, movements which are suggestive of breathing. In some cases the aura stretches considerably beyond the periphery of the clump and then contracts to a smaller size with a long, slow, rhythmic beat, but in others it appears to be almost a flutter, reminding one of the quick motion of a butterfly's wings. Striving to touch their consciousness when so engaged, I find that their idea seems to be to press closer to the heart or centre of the informing life of the flower. The fairy experiences great pleasure in this act, and has the feeling of having poured something of its own nature and vitality into the flowers. When it has done this it rises into the air and hovers in a condition of quietude and semi-repose, whilst its vitality is renewed.

By this time I have gained a more satisfactory entry into their world. The air contains very large numbers of them, and individuals descend and perform the act, which I have described, while others are seen rising after its completion. The average height to which they rise in the air must be somewhere about fifteen to twenty feet, though some mount much higher ; at the higher levels there is more lateral movement ; probably it is at this level, say eighty to 100 feet up, that they travel. The scene is indescribably beautiful, and the atmosphere of it enchanting. I cannot see that they have any other occupations than those described. They are, undoubtedly, very busy indeed at this period of the year. The one first described still waits near us, and, on closer inspection, I see the faintest suggestion of arms, but neither body, legs nor wings. The dense portion of the aura is probably about two feet six inches high.

In the Cotswolds. August 7th, 1925.

I have been very much interested in watching a nature-spirit who has been submitting us to the same kind of scrutiny which we are accustomed to turn upon her people.

She is a non-individualised deva, at a stage between the fairy and the sylph, possessing some of the characteristics of both.

Though she first appeared as we walked through the thick wood and is still hovering between the tops of the pine trees, upon which we are looking down, she does not seem to be definitely connected with the wood, and certainly is not attached, for purposes of work, to any tree or group of trees. I think she is a flower fairy who is passing onwards to an aerial life like that of the sylphs, and that the time of her individualisation is fast approaching. Her body is composed of the matter of the higher subplanes of the astral, very light, tenuous, and beautiful. The actual form and manner are those of a vivacious young school-girl. At the moment her aura closely resembles moving clouds of colour, through which waves and ripples of light pass continually at irregular intervals. She has gained a higher measure of stability than is possessed by the average fairy, and is evidently able to remain relatively motionless in mid-air for quite a long period of time. She sees our astro-mental selves quite clearly, but it requires some concentration for her to see the physical form, and even then her vision of it is very vague. Endeavouring to contact her consciousness, I perceive that she sees chiefly the astral double of all physical plane objects ; a tree, for example, appearing to her as a dark central form, which corresponds to the physical shape, interpenetrated and surrounded by a pale luminous grey light, which I presume is the etheric double, surrounded in its turn by a violet astral aura, extending about six inches beyond the physical form. To her, each tree is like an engine, into and through which force is flowing from the astral plane, vivifying and illuminating it—keeping it alive from her point of view ; and, of course, she is right, for without this it could not live. To her it is as though the tree were performing, in a much larger degree, a similar function to that which we attribute to the physical atom. She sees at the root of the tree, just below the ground level, a golden-coloured vortex of energy, where the force enters from the astral plane, and from which it passes throughout the whole body of the tree. She does not appear to know anything of the physical processes ; at any rate, she is not interested in them, being firmly convinced that they are secondary to the astral and relatively unimportant. If I may put her ideas into our language —she brushed away my references to the physical processes, saying : " It's the flow of the life forces that is important." She says that she *does* know about the physical plane processes more than we know, in fact, on their *life* side.

She is now trying to understand what the possession of a physical form means to us, and what it would mean to her. She exerts a " drawing " influence upon me, as if to try whether she can move my body. She thus draws out and stretches the front of my astral and mental bodies until they touch hers—she being fifteen yards away—but, try as she will, she cannot make any real impression upon the dense physical. Her consciousness, in relation to movement, is completely filled with the idea of the instantaneous response, which the matter of the subtler planes always makes to an act of will ; more so, in fact, in the deva than the human, for the matter of their subtler bodies seems to be more vital and electric than is ours. She has discovered that fact from the touch of my aura, which feels heavy to her. She holds a portion of it in contact with herself, and is examining it as one would a piece of cloth. By trying to unite our minds to some extent, I have succeeded in making it possible for her to feel the inertia of the physical body. It is far greater to her consciousness than it is to mine, it feels to her as a body of lead would feel to me.

Now she is jerking at the etheric in an endeavour to produce movement, and I am helping her to as close a contact with the dense physical body as possible. For a moment she feels panic-stricken, then a sensation of being buried, of hopeless imprisonment ; she makes very great efforts to lift the physical into the air, and this has the effect of stretching the etheric double of the body and filling it with light ; it also makes the physical feel a little lighter, producing that curious consciousness, which one sometimes has in dreams, that just a little effort would enable one to float. This very close contact with her feels to me as if it were loosening the association and lessening the cohesion of the atoms of my body. I should think that a powerful individualised deva could transmute the physical body into a kind of astral counterpart—perhaps that is what happens to changelings. She has withdrawn again, and is evidently profoundly affected by the experience. Among the many sensations it has produced in her is one of wonder, that we can endure such imprisonment perpetually. She does not appear to know about life and death, or even freedom during sleep ; I have tried to explain these things to her. Our life seems hopelessly complex, and she cannot understand how we could choose it in preference to the comparatively straightforward deva existence—for they do not lay the undue stress on " form " that we do. She says, " To be unable to spring free into the air, leap into the distance, flash across a valley, and to have to drag so wearily and slowly such a dull body, is worse than non-existence." Judging from her present state of mind, it does not appear at all likely that she will be one of those who will change from the deva to the human kingdom, but I must admit that to me the reverse is very tempting.

I tried just now to give her some conception of the Masters ; she, translating the idea into her own realm, thought of some kind of super-deva, some archangel leader of whose existence she seems to be aware. At that moment the deva of the valley appeared behind her, smiling and wonderful, in all his radiant beauty, and enfolded her in his aura, drawing her near to his left side. This filled her with great happiness and a sense of exaltation. She stayed but a moment and flashed off, exalted by the contact, springing free like some creature of the wilds. The relationship between them appears to resemble closely that between pupil and Master in the human kingdom.

In the mind of the deva of the valley, there seems to exist clear knowledge of the evolutionary stages through which his kingdom passes, and I rather think that it was he who put the fairy and myself in touch with each other, perhaps for our mutual education. He also is conscious of superiors, of the hierarchical order of his race. An endeavour to understand his conception turns my consciousness upwards into extra-terrestrial space. I hesitate to describe the vision which follows because, in bringing it through, I seem to have got it so materialised and debased.

I see a long table covered with a cloth of bright light, in the centre of which lies a cross. At both ends are seated great spiritual beings of the deva order. From either end a line of devas stretches back, rising higher and higher in the heavens till they are lost and only a dazzling splendour, and ineffable radiance, remains ; steps lead upwards from the table, and up and down them shining ones are passing. From the centre of the vision there is a continual outpouring of power, in wave after wave of delicate yet vivid colour ; golden and rose, it flows outwards and downwards, giving to the whole scene an effulgence and a splendour which is completely beyond my powers of description.

CHAPTER V

DURING a walk in Epping Forest, we found the stump of a tree which had been cut down, and out of the sides of which young shoots were growing. An attempt to understand the processes showed that connected with, and in some measure responsible for, each of the rose-coloured shoots was a nature-spirit, which acted as one of the final links in a chain of consciousness reaching up to the deva in charge of the vegetable kingdom ; it was more like a bee than a fairy, and it literally buzzed at me as I approached close to the shoots.

When the tree was cut down, the major part of the consciousness was withdrawn, yet, owing to the fact that the root was left in the ground and was still alive, some portion was left behind. The stump of a tree is not a particularly responsive medium, but when, in due season, the sensitive young shoots appeared, they provided a means of expression and expansion for the indwelling life ; though the evolving vegetable consciousness pervades every cell, there is also an astro-etheric centre in the middle of the stump, just below the ground level, where the roots begin to project, and which looks like a globe of yellow light, some four to six inches in diameter ; ripples flow out from it, giving it

38

the appearance of a large golden flower with pointed petals arranged in concentric circles, getting paler in colour in proportion to their distance from the centre.

At the heart of this " flower," force is constantly welling up into the etheric from the astral, forming a vortex which emits an etheric vibration ; this produces " sound," which is formative, and governs to a large extent the shape of any growth which takes place within its influence.

By a curious operation of Nature, when this vibration impinged upon my aura, it produced upon it a miniature tree-form, the archetype of the tree.

Apparently a process similar to this takes place in the consciousness of the builders of all degrees ; each one, according to his capacity and development, obtains in this way a realisation of the work which has to be done, both in colour and in form ; in the lower orders of nature-spirits this process is almost entirely instinctive, and is probably only self-conscious in the individualised deva. As physical growth continues, more and more of the vegetable consciousness is expressed, so that the vibrations from the centre become more complex ; new " notes " are added, each one calling the appropriate nature-spirit builder, vivifying the type of matter which corresponds to it, and producing the form into which that matter has to be built.

The vibratory range of this particular life-centre is at least twelve feet in all directions, and a specialised sphere is thus formed in which the various orders of builders concerned—called to the spot by the " note " which is the keynote of their own existence—find conditions which are perfect for the work they have to do. Arriving within this sphere, the builders materialise to the etheric level at which the work has to be done, absorb the matter which is vibrating at their own rate, and, having specialised it by contact with themselves, discharge it into the etheric mould or form, which is the expression of the vibration.

By this means, and by these agencies, the gradual growth of the tree takes place.

ON THE FUNCTIONS OF THE TREE-SPIRIT

A tree may be regarded as having a soul, because a portion of the monad-bearing life-wave pervades it,* and evolves by means of incarnation within it ; its evolution is quickened when a nature-spirit takes charge of a tree.† The first effect is the quickening of responsiveness in the dreaming consciousness of the tree. The brilliant corruscations of the aura of the nature-spirit play continuously upon the tree conscious-ness, forcing it, in the course of time, to a dim and dull reproduction within itself of these vibrations. The actual sensitiveness of the physical tree to impacts from without becomes increased, and with it the response of the consciousness to those impacts.

The nature-spirit, being so much more highly evolved, appears also to act as a link, or channel, for energies from higher levels of consciousness, and so fulfil a function which is a faint reflection of that of the ego in man, which is that of a lens, focus, or channel between spirit and matter. This is possible to the nature-spirit, because he has achieved a considerable measure of awakened self-consciousness, which is the essential factor.

* *Vide A Study in Consciousness*, by A. Besant.
† *Vide Fairies at Work and at Play*, by Geoffrey Hodson.

It may be said that each vegetable group-soul is in the charge of an advanced deva, under whom the tree-spirits work. This hierarchical system is in operation throughout the whole deva evolution right down to the fairies and form-builders, functioning in the vegetable kingdom, the whole being under the control of the group-soul deva. He, in his turn, serves and obeys some great archangel of our earth's vegetable kingdom, who, knowing the plan in the mind of the Logos, transmits his instructions through the various grades, down even to the tiny etheric creatures who build and inform the material structure.

It may be that the occupancy of a tree for a long period by a nature-spirit is a sacrifice, and forms a means of swifter unfoldment, a path of service, in fact. This, like all true sacrifice, will cause no real pain, though a sense of limitation must be present on the lower planes. In taking up its abode in a tree, the nature-spirit appears to unify itself with the complete cell life of the tree, thus making homogeneous that which was heterogeneous ; it, therefore, may be regarded as an expression of the soul of the tree, though at the same time it is a separate entity.

It will be seen from this how close is the relationship between nature-spirit and tree, and how the evolution of both is quickened by this intimate Pitri * function. Possibly on the death of such a tree, whether from age or the woodman's axe, the nature-spirit, released from its association, gathers up within itself the evolutionary results of the life of the tree and provides conditions, in which a process of gestation may take place, faintly corresponding to those of devachanic and causal

* Vide The Building of the Cosmos, by A. Besant.

human consciousness. Whether that particular sum
total of experience is released throughout the vegetable
group-soul or is conserved, and reincarnated with the
same nature-spirit in attendance, I am unable to say,
though I think the latter a possibility in cases of highly-
advanced vegetable consciousness. One wonders
whether a nature-spirit might not choose to see the
embryo soul through into the animal kingdom, and
even into the human. We do not know how far back
our relationship to the nature-spirit world may not be
traced.

CHAPTER VI

BROWNIES AND MANNIKINS

Petit Salève, near Geneva. June 1st, 1925.

THE brownies hereabout are dressed in much brighter colours than any I have seen in England. There are great numbers on the hillside, most of whom wear bright crimson hats of the peaked variety, a light russet brown coatee and breeches; their faces are broad; they are all bearded, and have little black, beady eyes. Their bodies are rather flat and broad, and their legs are wide apart where they leave the trunk. They have large rough hands and very gruff voices.

As I watch I see a little troop of them come up the hillside; some carry satchels with straps over their shoulders; others, tiny picks with brightly-polished heads; in some cases these are carried with the handle slipped through the belt, in others in the right hand. There are thirty or forty in this troop, which climbs the hill quite slowly and apparently with some effort. They talk in low guttural voices to each other, much as workmen would on their way to their tasks, and there are distinct variations in character to be noticed amongst them. They are not all gruff—some are quite jovial, and such an one has withdrawn from the group and approached us. He stands some twenty or thirty

43

feet away, legs wide apart, hands on hips, and looks up at us with face beaming with good temper, with which is mingled a certain self-conceit, as if he would say : " Here am I ; take a good look at me. Am I not a wonderful fellow ? " He stretches out his right hand and points to the hills and country beyond, as much as to say " All this is mine ; is it not a wonderful home ? " I asked him to come nearer, and he walked up to within six feet of us, but the moment our astral emanations began to touch him he lost all his self-assurance, his form began to lose its definition, all his jollity disappeared, he became confused, and began to lose his sense of personal identity. He stepped back and hurriedly ran away, joining the troop, which had now passed on up the hillside. This one was hatless and wore a leather apron like a blacksmith, fastened by a tightly buckled belt, in which a few tiny blacksmith's tools could be seen. I could make out a tiny pair of pincers and a little hammer.

He has now returned, having almost recovered his composure, and, standing partly behind a bush, looks up at us roguishly, but with much less self-assurance. The strutting swagger which characterised him at first has completely vanished ; then he was actuated by motives of self-conceit, and wished to show himself off to us, but now he returns from curiosity and a certain feeling of attraction towards us. It is interesting to notice that the tools and the belt have lost their definition, their outline is only faintly traceable in a mass of the raw material from which they were created and which is still visible, adhering to him at the place where the tools were.

As I watch him I see that his self-confidence is

rapidly returning ; he begins to feel more sure of himself, and has stepped out from behind the bush ; once
more he approaches, but not so near as at the first
time ; he is just the same height as the long grasses,
i.e., about one foot six inches.

To my surprise he suddenly begins to sing ; he has a
deep baritone voice and his song consists of a repetition
of the words, " Ho, ro, ro, ro," and appears to be
expressive of the joys of the brownie existence ; at its
level it reflects much the same sentiment as does, " A
Life on the Ocean Wave " ; in fact, I was immediately
reminded of this song. There are only four notes—
G E C A—but these are repeated on the descending
scale in the same relationship, with varying time value
at each repetition. He gesticulates with his hand
while singing, pointing to the different aspects of the
scenery. An attempt to unite my consciousness with
his shows me that he cannot really see across the valley
which separates the Grand Salève from the Petit
Salève ; in fact, his whole conception of the landscape
is limited, and the grasses shut him in very much ; but
he has a strong sense of direction and seems to establish
a sort of *rapport* with the place to which he is moving.

He has disappeared now, but a number of other little
men are watching us with a timid sort of curiosity.
They belong to a different family. They have fresh
and youthful faces and are smaller and slimmer than
the brownies, so that they should be classed with the
mannikins. They wear green scalloped coatees edged
with yellow, which hang loosely over the hips. They
belong to a lower order of development than the
brownies, being much less self-conscious. These little
people live among the grasses and are only about

six inches high. They scamper about among the roots, and also make short flights. They seem to be intimately associated with, and inseparable from, the grass —almost to be, in fact, its life-side made objective. It would be interesting to know what happens to them when the hay is cut. I should say that they will fade out of objective existence till the grass grows again.

We are sitting with our backs against a stone wall built into the hillside to prevent landslips. Over the top of this a number of brownies are peering down on us, and we seem to cause them a good deal of excitement. There is quite a flutter in their ranks. One old gentleman is particularly daring and seems to have an unusually well-knit and stable body, for though he is immediately behind and above our heads, he seems able to maintain his equilibrium without much difficulty. He is a red-faced and jolly old greybeard and keeps on passing items of information about us to the more timorous members of the group behind him. Some do not even dare to approach the edge, while others just peep over and start back quickly. As I describe this the numbers are increasing, till there is quite a crowd on the little plateau above us ; they seem to be holding a kind of council meeting, as well as awaiting the return of those who continue to watch us quite closely. I see now that the " greybeard " is the one whom I noticed as being the leader of the troop when I first saw it coming up the hill. He wears a long brown coat which reaches to his feet. He looks older than the others, and is undoubtedly superior, both in intelligence and self-control, to any of the rest, and they appear to acknowledge his leadership. He has some dim conception of the existence of grades in

his order, and knows that he is responsible for carrying
out the wishes of a superior, and his guidance of a tribe
and his life generally is more self-conscious and less
instinctive than theirs.   At the same time he is very
childish ; he has adopted an air of great superiority
(as one who is familiar with these higher beings,
meaning ourselves !), and the attitude of one to whom
some homage is due, as a result of his ability to gaze
unhindered upon us.   He seems to have no consciousness of difference of sex ; while he sees that my wife
differs from me, *i.e.*, that her hair is long and curly, he
cannot understand that while obviously belonging to
the same tribe we should have such strongly marked
difference of appearance.   My khaki shirt and flannels
are well within his grasp, being not too unlike what he
is accustomed to, but my wife's frock is something new
and utterly strange in his experience.   Our large size,
too, fills him with amazement, and it is evident that
though there are houses and farms dotted about in the
valley below, and men and women working in the field,
he has never before had a plain view of humankind.   He
would be vaguely aware of their existence, associating
them with the place in which he happened to
find them, and regarding that place as pleasant or
unpleasant, dimly seeing something large, but not dis-
sociating it from the place.   His present experience
is giving him a decided thrill, and his little body is
trembling with the strain of the close contact which he
is at last beginning to find too much for him ; it has
given him a very much widened outlook, and he will
never be quite the same again.   He reminds me of a
human being who has seen a great vision which he can
never forget, and it seems probable that before long

he will break free from the limitation of the brownie existence and enter a state wherein he will find wider fields of consciousness.

We started to ask a blessing upon him, but this proved too much and his form began to disintegrate, so we desisted, and he now lies on the hillside slowly recovering, whilst his younger brethren crowd around. Consciousness quickly returns, and he sits up, still with the vacant expression of one who sees a vision, and from his appearance it would seem that even his joyous existence has been made a little more intensely happy and that when he finally settles down he will indeed be the better for the contact.

Time calls us away and we leave the brownies with their guttural and excited chatter still ringing in our ears and a decided feeling that we, too, have gained something from this experience, which has given us a closer sense of kinship with the fairies, and has made them appear still more lovable in our eyes.

In a Thick Beechwood in the Cotswolds.
August 9th, 1925.

There are hundreds of small brown mannikins playing about on the thick carpet of the leaves of past seasons with which the ground under the trees is covered. They are from eight to twelve inches high, and vary in colour from the grey-green of the beech trunks to the rich brown of the dead leaves. Contact with them immerses one in an exceedingly curious atmosphere. They have the faces of very old men combined with a childish mentality and the antics and movements of little boys. They wear coats and knee breeches of a material which looks like brown beech bark; they have long pointed feet and some wear tiny boots. A feature of their attire which is novel to me is the head-dress; this is like a cowl which lies in loose folds on the shoulders, enveloping the whole head with the exception of the face, and hangs loosely down behind, where it ends in a point. They have grey eyebrows, mustachios and beards; these last are, in some cases, cut square, in others more or less pointed. Their quaintness is further added to by their facial expression, which is one of intent seriousness and earnestness—all about nothing. At first glance one might think that they were very important people, but in looking into what corresponds to their minds, one finds almost a complete blank. Again, I notice that peculiar sense of repetition, as of one who is continually repeating the same sentence to himself.

They appear to " live " inside the trees, into which there are accepted entrances. These are generally small hollows in the trunk, frequently, though not always, level with the ground. There are groups which appear to live up in the forks, where the branches leave the main trunk. Though they can move for short distances in the air, they seem to prefer to run up the trunks of the trees. This they do as easily as if they ran upon the flat ground. They seem to be unaffected by the laws of gravity, for they maintain a horizontal position as they pass up and down with their bodies at right-angles to the trunks. Although their forms are a homogeneous solid without interior organisation, a close observation of their movements seems to indicate something corresponding to a muscular system; this is particularly noticeable when they jump, as they often do for short distances; for example, the last half yard of their journey back to their tree is often covered by a leap. The leg with which the take-off is made certainly seems to harden and stiffen, to relax during flight, and both legs to be braced up for the landing ; on the other hand, landing is perfectly smooth, and the forward movement continues at practically the same speed.

Several of these little gentlemen have been demonstrating for our benefit, so that even the non-clairvoyant members of their human audience saw the movements of the leaves which they made, though the etheric agents were invisible to them. They seem to grow old, for the chief variation in their appearance is that of age. Just now a doddering and very decrepit little old man walked up the hill, with the air of one who comes to see what all the disturbance is about. He did not look up from the ground until he was within about four yards of us, then he saw us ; when whatever impression he was capable of receiving had sunk in, he was visibly staggered. Evidently we are something entirely new in his experience, and it is amusing to see the air of importance and childish *aplomb* disappear, giving place to amazement ; he staggers backwards a few feet, and his eyes protrude in a manner which would surely be alarming to his friends ! The intensity of his surprise however, soon passes of, and he steps a little nearer and then moves round to the front of us in order to get a better view. Whatever his other emotions may have been, he certainly shows no fear ; he seems to be conscious of, and to like the incense which we are burning.

Though at first I doubted the accuracy of my observation, I now see beyond all doubt that he supports himself with a stick in just the same way as a very aged human would do. He now sits down, settling

himself for a thorough inspection. A short and sudden
rainfall demonstrates to me that he is in no way affected
by it. Another surprise has awaited him. He now
finds that there are three members of our party instead
of one as he at first supposed. The lady who is sitting
a little apart, offers him a further field for speculation ;
he does not appear to be able to connect her with us ;
to him she is an independent phenomenon as completely
outside his experience as we are, and equally beyond his
comprehension. She now strikes a match to light
another stick of incense and he is so astonished that he
actually leaps from the ground and withdraws, placing
a further three feet between us. It is curious to see him
rise in the air a distance of six inches or so involuntarily,
still retaining his sitting posture ! Again he creeps
forward to his old position, using his hands as a means
of propulsion.

The effect of our auras upon him is interesting. His
little astral body, which consists of a shapeless and
almost colourless cloud, smaller if anything than the
etheric, is beginning to glow ; this produces a warm,
comfortable feeling inside him which he likes very
much ; in other words, our presence stimulates him.
He begins to lose his feeling and also his appearance of
extreme old age—the change of consciousness, finding
expression in the rather childish grin which slowly
spreads over his face. Now he grows bolder and
approaches to within eight feet of us, appearing to be
specially attracted towards the lady. After a few
minutes, he has lost his appearance of old age and is
prancing up and down before her as if to show off. He
twirls his stick, stopping every now and then to bow
towards her with his hand on his middle. A most

curious thing has now happened to him ; as he was bowing, he bent his body forward from the hips so deeply, that he reached the horizontal position and suddenly saw the leaves and brown earth, when he promptly forgot all about us ; on looking up after about half a minute of contemplation, he received the staggering shock of our presence all over again ! This time it was evidently too much for him, and he quickly retired to some distance, taking cover in the grass which grows at the edge of the wood.

A great number of his brethren have gradually become aware of our presence and, gathered in a semicircular crowd, are observing us from within the wood. Some are sitting still as if transfixed, others walk up and down and appear to be addressing remarks to their seated fellows as they pass them ; others make little exploratory journeys in our direction, retiring as our auras become too much for them. Again I see the little man previously described ; he is still young in appearance, visibly excited, and keeps repeating something to himself. He seems to have some difficulty in remaining on the ground ; he keeps rising and falling just above the grasses, as though his body, becoming unstable, was temporarily out of his control. Upon the others the chief effect which we seem to produce is a general quickening of all their faculties. Though the comparison is not a nice one, the effect is much like that of alcohol upon one unaccustomed to it ! Though it may, and surely will, die down, it will leave some permanent mark upon them—producing a decided quickening of their evolution.

In fact, as the place upon which we are sitting has been used frequently for various investigations and has become magnetised, it will probably have a peculiar and, we may hope, beneficial effect upon all the members of the elemental kingdom within the sphere of its influence. Though we are quite ordinary from the human point of view, we are most extraordinary from mannikin standards—as great an evolutionary distance separating us from them, as separates us from, say, the mighty Chohans of the Great White Lodge.

The Cotswolds. August 23rd, 1925.

The rays of the evening sun are falling upon a grassy hillside at the edge of the wood and this has attracted large numbers of nature-spirits—some of them from the wood—who are to be seen amusing themselves after the manner of their kind. There are at least three distinct species of mannikin and quite a number of fairies. Altogether they make a charming spectacle. Amongst them there are some little tree-men similar to those previously described, some brownies, and some small green people who probably belong to the grass. On closer examination I find that the tree-mannikins differ in many ways from those seen under the beeches, the wood in this part being mainly composed of larch. They are younger, thinner, and much more sprightly. They have very thin faces, sharp features and pointed noses ; they wear a long pointed cap which falls down the back when they are walking and streams behind them when they float. The dress consists of a tight-fitting coat and nether garments, and their legs end in rather long feet beyond which their stockings pass to a point. This loose point is something new to me in fairy dress and must be rather inconvenient, for when they are moving on the ground it frequently gets turned under the foot ; I do not see that it impedes progress, however. The colouring of the clothes is dark brown with touches of green here and there, the amount of which varies with individuals ; in some the long cap is all green, in others all brown ; there are also some whose colour is somewhere between the two. The height of these little men is about eighteen inches.

One of their chief amusements is to " run " swiftly down the hillside till they are within about twenty yards of the wood, to leap forward, passing swiftly through the air, skimming the top of the wall at the edge of the wood, and coming down some twenty or thirty yards on the other side. They look very quaint as they " fly " through the air with their caps streaming behind, their feet stretched out before them, the long points of their stockings being extended beyond the toes. Some of them are passing up and down the hill swiftly, with giant strides, and it seems evident that the swift passage through the sunlit air affords them great pleasure. Weak though the rays of the sun are at this time of day, they do not appear to be able to bear them for very long, finding it necessary to return at frequent intervals to the shade which the woods afford. Evidently they are not accustomed to the full strength of the actinic rays, whose power is, of course, much reduced under trees where they live. There is, therefore, a reason for the swift flights into the wood, which I noticed from the first ; but, though they are a necessity, they are also a source of pleasure.

The brownies are much heavier in build and more jocosely bucolic in temperament ; they are very fat little men, about a foot high, in the traditional brownie clothing, many of them wearing a large square brass buckle to fasten their belts in front. There is a short cape to their coats, which has a scalloped edge and is faced with yellow, the rest of the clothing being brown. They also have pointed caps of normal length. They have fresh complexions and heavy brown beards and mustachios. Most of their faces wear broad smiles. They are trotting about in twos and threes, and some are playing ring games. Their dances are somewhat like the rather clumsy endeavours of the old-time rustic ; it is amusing to see them hasten their speed by floating, without apparently being aware of the fact. I have just watched one cross the field ; he started by walking, this developed into a kind of trot, after which he rose some six inches above the ground and floated swiftly for thirty or forty yards, still keeping up the running motion of his legs, which he continued after he had landed ; finally he fell into a walk before stopping.

There is some form of communication between them going on all the time, for I see—but do not hear—much shouting of one to another, with a great deal of expressive gesture. They have very little individuality, the consciousness in all of them being practically the same. They really have nothing to communicate to each other because they all represent one consciousness, which is playing more or less equally through them all. The keynote of that consciousness is happiness, and that, for the time being, is also the prevailing trait of the forms through which it is manifesting.

In a similar way the tiny green mannikins, from four to six inches high, appear to be expressions of a consciousness intimately associated with the grass. They have chubby little children's faces, and the rest of their form appears to consist of green material, so that they are clothed in tight-fitting one-piece suits, and caps from which their small pointed ears protrude slightly.

Eerde Woods. Star Camp. July 27th, 1926.

Last night after " camp fire " we walked away from the camp and deeper into the pine wood. The sun was setting in a crimson glow, which lit up the clouds and shone between the dark stems of the trees. The sense of the presence of the Lord, which had been so real throughout the day, reached its culmination round the camp fire, and the final chanting of the peace man-trams induced a state of poise throughout the bodies, giving us tranquillity of soul.

We came to a small fir-clad hill which we climbed, and, seated at the top, we looked ahead into the dark recesses of the woods.

The influence of the camp spreads far and wide throughout the country, and it seemed that at this short distance the nature-spirits had been sharing in our happiness. There was an air of happiness and of gentleness about them, as though the spirit of universal love had, for a time, tamed their nature and rendered them more than usually responsive to human feelings of affection. The eyes of the sylphs did not burn with such a fierceness, the gnomes and brownies seemed less weird and other-worldly, and none started or withdrew at our approach. Our auras were glowing with the power and the blessing which pervade the camp in which we live, sleep, meditate, take our food, play our games, and do our work. Perhaps, being lifted above our normal selves, nearer to our real selves by His presence, we had also been brought nearer to these denizens of the woods, these members of the devic hosts ; for, as we sat silently, each living in the world of his own happy dreams, the world of ecstasy and happiness supreme, into which our Head continually lifted us, many orders of nature-spirits drew near.

The woods hereabouts contain a white-and-brown clothed tribe of brownie. They are some six or eight inches in height, broad and squat of figure, with heavy dark-bearded faces, white jerkins and brown knicker-bockers, stockings and boots, the only variation among them being in the colour of the pointed cap, which ranged through the different colours of the spectrum. These quaintly serious little fellows stood in the hollow below us occasionally looking up as if discussing us, with each other; gradually some of them walked towards us, with a curious rocking motion of their bodies from side to side. As they drew near they felt the influence of the Star about us, and they bathed in our auras.

One member of the party possesses a ring which has been powerfully magnetised and linked to one of the Elder Brethren, and as she held her hands forward inviting the nature-spirits to come nearer, the power of the ring sprayed downwards at her feet, enveloping one of the brownies, who had drawn nearer than the rest ; at first he experienced a distinct shock and withdrew from the stream and partly faded out of the etheric world into the astral, his etheric form becoming vague and indistinct ; as he recovered himself he realised that, apart from the first shock, the experience had been distinctly pleasant, stimulating him and giving him a sense of expansion and of increased vitality. He then re-assumed his brownie form, stepped into the current of force and proceeded to indulge in a shower bath, strutting about within the area of the influence of the ring, throwing up his arms and doing his best to absorb as much of the force as he could.   Other members of his family also came very near, even walking between us as we sat, though in every case it appeared to take them some little time to adjust themselves to us. With astral vision they were clearly visible in their brownie forms, but at the physical level they showed only as points of light, tiny clouds of colour with occasional gleams of their white jerkins; the mossy ground below us was covered with these moving flashes of light.

CHAPTER VII

THE KINGDOM OF PAN

Petit Salève, near Geneva. June 1st, 1925.

WE are lying high up on the hillside, having strolled out from our hotel, which stands about 2,000 feet high, and ascended the steep slope of the Petit Salève. It is a gloriously sunny day, and as we look upon the verdant valley and magnificent ranges of mountains topped by Mont Blanc in the distance, the scene seems almost too wonderful to be true.

Many "little folk" of delightful and fascinating character are to be seen all about us on the slopes of the hill. There is a charming and rather venturesome species of fairy which, though childlike and naïve, has also a decidedly mischievous trait. There are numbers of small fauns, too, true to type except that they have the faces of children instead of swarthy bearded men. Also there is a more highly evolved kind of nature-spirit which must be approaching individualisation. These last are unusually placid and sedate in their nature and expression. They are all-white creatures of human height and appearance ; they float slowly across the valleys, through the gardens and up and down the slopes of the hills, pausing often in their flight to allow their soft and gentle gaze to rest upon their human brothers ; they appear to take interest in them, but in a detached way, with much the same attitude of mind in which we gaze at familiar animals behind the bars of their cages in the Zoological Gardens.

There are also jolly little brownies, merry and serious by turns, now very busy with some important activity, now playing irresponsibly, sometimes forming rings and squares, sometimes tumbling and rolling, and, again, taking long jumping flights, accompanied by grotesque and ridiculous contortions and gestures.

By these and others, we were accompanied as we walked slowly up the hillside, and all around us was a ceaseless chatter and excited gambolling, as we climbed the hill. Now, as we sit down to watch them, some have seated themselves around us, while others play about in the near vicinity. Their presence gives the place a fairylike enchantment and beauty, and produces feelings of great happiness, which might almost be called bliss if there were not an irresponsible gaiety associated with it. Nothing matters in the very least, time does not exist, one place is as good as another. As there is neither purpose nor pain, nor any unsatisfied desire, there is nothing to be done but centre the whole of one's nature in the enjoyment, the happiness of being alive.

The fauns are by far the quietest and most serious of all the little folk. They have the faces and bodies of children of five or six years old, dark curly hair, pointed ears, bare arms and trunks, shaggy little legs and the cloven hoof of the animal. There is a certain peculiar secretiveness and slyness about them, as though they were always carrying out some plot. Their eyes are elongated and sly in expression, as they look out through half-opened lids. The little tail is short, perhaps three inches long, and curls upwards ; the height is about eighteen inches to two feet.   In some cases, though not in all, the skin is swarthy, and some look more sunburnt than others.   Their arms are strong and used for climbing, and by their aid they pull themselves into the branches of the small trees and up the rocks. They move about with a curious trotting pace, upright on their hind feet.

Closer contact shows them to have a special atmosphere of their own, quite different from that of any other members of the fairy kingdom which I have hitherto observed.   One's mind is taken back to primeval ages, as if to the springtime of the whole planet,when all the world was young.   There is a peculiar vibration emanating from these little creatures, unlike either the human or the fairy, as if they belonged to a third stream which had its origin deep in the bowels of the earth.

Allowing the consciousness to travel backwards in time in search of deeper understanding, scenes strange and weird appear.   Huge creatures of gigantic proportions sit brooding, chin in hand, elbow on knee, on ledges of rock.   They are neither ape nor man, nor elemental, but possess something of the characteristics of all three ; they are some fifteen to twenty feet in height ; they possess a powerful instinctive mentality which lifts them far beyond the intellectual level of any known animal, yet it is rather an intensification of instinct than a development towards the reasoning mentality of man. They appear to belong to a stratum below that which is at present manifest on earth, to a branch of the elemental kingdom where consciousness is a reflection below what we know as personal consciousness, a third triad. Diagrammatically these might be represented by an upward pointed triangle with its apex touching that of the downward pointed triangle which represents the personality, and its base far down below in a region of consciousness which appears to belong to the remote and unknown past of evolution. We have passed so far beyond that stage, that I have no means of contacting it and no principle within myself through which I can study it; an endeavour to push past the form brings me to a complete blank, a yawning chasm of nothingness, from which arise no ideas, no conceptions, as if I had reached the downward limit of consciousness and could press no further; neither does an intense effort of will assist me. I simply cannot " tune in " to that unknown and apparently unknowable rate of vibration. I cannot even feel a vibration from it; yet, whenever I try to push past the form, to what in present-day evolution would be a subtler, higher principle, I feel my consciousness to be pointed definitely downward. The whole phenomenon is curious in the extreme and calls for several changes of attitude in endeavouring to understand it; for instance, in our present evolution, the form of a person or thing is its densest expression, its heaviest encasement; with these creatures, the form is the highest and least dense expression, as if the innermost was objective and the outermost subjective, which, as will be seen, is a complete reversal of the present system.

One assumes that this state of affairs must be capable of continuance indefinitely, just as the upward trend of the present is capable of being pursued into infinite heights, until one reaches a point where the two are one, and the circle of being complete. Be that as it may, the satyrs and fauns appear to have their origin in, and to be the last remnant of, a more deeply involved stream of consciousness, and it is this, perhaps, which gives them their peculiarly weird and unusual vibration.

As a result of the endeavour described above, the other types of nature-spirits now appear to me to be very new, like a freshly-painted picture with the pigment still moist and glistening. There appears to be little or no communication between them and the fauns, and one gets the impression that, though geographically together, they are really living in different worlds.

There are large numbers of these fauns, and they look very strange when twenty or thirty of them scamper up the hillside, their bare backs gleaming and their little hoofs padding over the grassy slope.

Whilst I have been describing this, I have been sub-consciously aware of being watched by a " person " whom I first took to be a discarnate human. His gaze interrupted me when I first began these observations, and I tried to drive him off without success—though, after the effort, I no longer felt any interference. I now see that he is not a human being, but is another of the creatures of Pan. I cannot see his feet at present, nor could I, till just now, see the top of his head, and he looked just like an ordinary man in dark clothes with a very hairy face and a long beard, over which he passes his hand. At the same time he feels weird, and I now see that the top of his head is covered with a growth of shaggy hair and that he has two short horns, one on either side of his forehead. He knows that I have made this discovery and there is a gleam in his eye and a sardonic smile upon his face, as he stands leaning carelessly against a tree trunk with his legs crossed. He will not move, he will not communicate, he just stands there taking pleasure in my inability to make anything of him and watching us with a curiously detached, yet amused interest. He is now taunting me with my failure, but, since he has shown even this activity, I have gained a clue. Once more I see that the consciousness is seated below the form and not above. There is something masterful about him, and he seems to be quite at home and superior to his environment. Beyond that I see and feel nothing. There is a complete blank.

The Same Place. *June 2nd*, 1925.

Note by a Deva

" The kingdom of Pan is slowly passing away, as far as human consciousness on this planet is concerned. It is a remnant of a period buried deep in the night of time, belonging, indeed, to a previous epoch. Some of its more promising members are given the opportunity of entering the human kingdom, and he whom you described was such an one, and the thought of what lay before him was in his mind, as he stood appraising you as members of the kingdom which he is about to enter.

When you exercise your ability to pierce the veil which generally hides the fairy people from men, it has the effect of opening a way also from their side, so that they, too, can see you more clearly. As you work, studying fairy life and exercising your clairvoyance, certain forces are brought into play, which they see as a radiance enveloping you ; and it is this which attracts their attention and causes them to stop and scrutinise you, in the way which you have so often noticed.

Though normally the nature-spirit is not interested in human beings, he is instinctively attracted to any one of them who shows special interest and understanding, particularly when that one is able to see him—a phenomenon which is sufficiently unusual to arrest his attention.

Further, from the higher ranks of the devic hierarchy an impulse is being sent forth similar to that which is noticeable on the human side, so that the deva and even the fairy consciousness begins to respond instinctively to the idea of closer co-operation ; they are much more responsive to such impulses than are humans, but their response is more collective than individual ; in fact, all the levels below that of individualisation evolve under a system which corresponds fairly closely to that of the group-soul, while above that level the community sense manifests to a very great degree. The commands of the deva hierarchy are always very readily obeyed, and full co-operation from the highest archangel down to the smallest of the builders can nearly always be obtained. There have been cases where a group has conceived the idea of making experiments of its own, and some of the more unpleasant of your insects and weeds are the result."

The Cotswolds. August 14th, 1925.

That the race of fauns has not died out in England is apparent from the fact that numbers of them are to be seen on the open hillside, at the end of the great beech wood, which grows on the slopes of the valley.

With slight differentiations, they appear to be formed upon the classical model. The upper part is that of a young boy, while, from the thigh downwards the body resembles the hind quarters of a shaggy-haired quadruped with the cloven hoof. The hair is thicker and less smooth than that of the goat ; there is a short tail curled slightly upwards. The expression of the face is utterly non-human, while it also differs from that of any member of the deva kingdom which I have seen. Beneath the curly hair, which covers the head, two dazzling and bold dark eyes glitter with an unearthly light. In addition to the eyebrows slanting slightly upwards, the modelling of the eye-socket also curves upwards at the outside, and it is this, together with their strange expression, which gives them their unearthly appearance.

They ' feel ' and look far more like the creatures of another world and another time, than do any of the fairy people. To human understanding, the combination of a child-body and a fully developed and mature intelligence is uncanny. They have a habit of stamping with their feet, as they stand in little knots and groups, between their wild scampers up and down the hillside. Several stand at the edge of the grass some twenty yards away with their wild eyes fixed upon us. Then one will give a start, paw the ground, and run with swift steps to the hill-top, joining several others who, standing thigh deep in the waving grasses, are outlined against the sky.

Again the phenomenon observed at Geneva presents itself. An attempt to touch the consciousness, as being above and subtler than the body, fails. The search yields a blank. Again the mind appears to plunge downwards, as if deep into the earth, and there finds itself surrounded by appearances like those of the old Pan world of Greek mythology. Here, deep in the

earth, as well as far below the normal levels of consciousness, exists the whole world of Pan, apparently a third
kingdom neither human nor devic, a kingdom of strange
shapes and weird forms, of man-headed animals and of
animal-headed men. This realm is so strange to me,
that I find exact and clear vision almost impossible as
yet. Certain human preconceptions have to be set
aside completely. The region below the surface is
neither dark nor solid, nor is it enclosed as the human
mind might expect by the surface of the earth. It is
lighted, but by no physical luminary. There is an
appearance of solidity, upon which trampling hoofs
can walk, yet there are levels above and below that,
which are also solid underfoot to their own inhabitants.
Here I see centaurs, though I cannot estimate their
size. They may be diminutive or they may be huge, I
cannot say which. They have the bodies of perfectly
moulded white horses, while above the shoulders, in
place of the horse's neck, there arises the torso and
head of a man. The skin is white, the hair is dark, the
face is bearded, and they seem to communicate in a
guttural language, and their speech is interspersed with
deep rolling laughter. Surely they must be huge in
size, for the sound issues in the tones of a thunderous
bass ; and yet, if I return to physical consciousness for
a moment, how small they look, like carved ivory
models set upon a shelf !

Everything seems inverted here, for from the depths
I can also see and hear the fauns scampering at the
surface of the earth, which looks like a surface, although
seen from far below it ; it is exactly as if people walked
and were audible and visible on the other side of the
great arch of the sky.

How crafty and cunning is the leer of the old satyrs as they crouch, full grown and swarthy, in their dens ! The idea of a den suggests an opening into something, yet though they appear to be encaved, there is no wall or indeed any solid matter behind them. Their eyes burn with a strange green fire—one sees it as a ray issuing from the eye, and visible for some distance along the line of vision. Again I receive the sense of extreme antiquity and a strange realisation that, behind all this, there is one consciousness, one being, of whom it is the objective representation ; though all these forms seem solid at first, they are evanescent, the temporary projections of a mind, which dwells far down in the earth. There is but one mind behind them all, which is the source of the strange intelligence shining through the eyes of the centaur and the satyr, as well as of the little fauns sent forth to play upon the surface of the earth.

A FRIENDLY FAUN

The Cotswolds. August 15th, 1925.

One of the fauns at my request has come quite close, and, as I dictate, stands by my right side. His presence has a peculiar effect on my etheric double, causing something like a shudder to pass through it, and, for a moment, the right side of my body seems to go cold. He exhales a faint odour, unusual though not unpleasant, something like that of freshly-ploughed earth.

The texture of his skin is beautifully smooth, and its colour like that produced in a swarthy man after a course of sun-bathing ; the eyes are wonderfully lustrous, and, in the case of this particular visitor, limpid and soft, for the time being, rather like those of an animal, though one feels, lurking quite near the surface of the consciousness, that unearthly weirdness mentioned before.

The eye is formed exactly like a human eye, though it is somewhat larger in proportion to the face. The eyelashes are long and curl upwards, and the hair of the eyebrows is dark and close. The forehead is beautifully modelled, and on either side, just above the hair line, protrude the two tiny horns, smooth and shiny, and of a rich dark brown colour. He allows me to touch them and to stroke his head (astrally), and the caress evidently gives him pleasure, for he rubs his head backwards and forwards against my hand. The hair is thicker and coarser than human hair and clusters round the head in loose curls. The nipples of the breast and the navel are clearly to be seen, and the body is rounded and shapely. As I caress while describing him, he becomes drowsy, and his outline vague and indistinct ; he begins to melt away, and then suddenly recalls himself, opens his eyes, and the outline of his form once more becomes clear. He shows the same kind of affection for me, as would an animal under similar circumstances. His cheeks are chubby and very soft to the touch. Nose, mouth, teeth and tongue are fully formed ; the body, however, is relatively hollow, only the outer shape to a depth of about two inches having been solidified ; I cannot tell whether it is warm or cold, because these conditions do not appear to have a correspondence on the astral plane. The experience is peculiar in many ways. For example, he has no aura that I can discern, unless the faint misty light which surrounds and interpenetrates him can be so designated. He has shown no powers of speech, or any ability to communicate up to now, beyond the responsiveness previously described, and certain corresponding changes of expression in the face.

He is now becoming a little restive, keeps looking towards his companions on the hillside, then to me. Although this might be interpreted as a request for permission to depart, I do not receive any mental communication to that effect. Possibly the body itself has a certain instinctive consciousness, from which these gestures proceed, rather than from an incarnated thinking entity. In spite of this conclusion, I continually receive the impression of a powerful intelligence operating *through* the form, yet also being completely detached ; it makes no sign of activity or change, but continues to shine through the eyes, giving far more an impression of power and strangeness than of intellect. This expression is exactly the same in all the fauns assembled here, and looking at them *en masse*, one feels that they all belong to one body— like the hairs on a head ; that although they vary slightly in appearance, and considerably in their antics and poses, yet they are all projections of one mind, the manifestation of one entity ; as though this being were somewhere deep down in the earth, and without himself moving, manifested his existence and power of motion through and by these forms, which are the projections of his consciousness, or an externalisation of his subconscious.

Perhaps the kingdom of Pan will prove to be part of the content of the subconscious mind of the Spirit of the Earth.

TREE CONSCIOUSNESS

The Cotswolds. August 18th, 1925.

Just as every animal, during incarnation, is an individual, if only a temporary one, so every tree, during its life, develops an individuality of its own. The great old beeches in this valley have developed distinct individuality, and do possess a sense of being, a faint form of self-consciousness.

Contact with this feeling of individuality produces a strange sensation, as if one were in the presence of huge motionless entities, each conscious of itself as separate from the rest, each possessing a certain amount of awareness, each having a definite atmosphere and exerting a definite influence. Once one gets past the physical body of the tree, a personality is met, and its consciousness can be touched. When just now a light breeze stirred the woods, arousing the whispering rustle of the beech and sending it sighing from end to end of the wood, the tree consciousness was aware of its arrival.

Entirely new sensations are produced in my consciousness, as I touch their inner life and enter to some slight degree the tree kingdom ; it is like stepping into a foreign country, seeing quite a new kind of people, and being adjusted to a new set of values. I feel that these " people " are very sensitive to the moods of Nature, the changes of weather and the seasons, and that they certainly possess sufficient consciousness to recognise them. One might say that they felt and recognised the evening breeze, in a kind of consciousness which would say to itself, " Ah, here is the evening breeze; how pleasant its touch as it sets my branches

swaying and my trunk swinging and my leaves a-
rustle." I almost dare say that it looks over to its
nearest neighbours to say, " Here it comes again."

This consciousness pervades every branch and every
root of the tree, though its centre seems to be in the
main trunk ; it seems sensitive to the very tips of the
branches, so that every movement of the leaves and
outermost twigs sends a thrill through some embryo
nervous system, some astral line of *rapport*, along
which the sensation reaches the central consciousness.
In the case of the beeches, the impression one receives
is decidedly of a male personality, and I find myself
continually thinking of them as tree-men. A still
closer contact reveals the presence of some kind of
inward urge towards growth, which I can most aptly
translate as a desire to stretch ; as if the divine
will, which is ever pressing forward along the evolutionary path, manifests itself in this way in the tree
consciousness, so that the " tree-man " feels a desire to
push himself further and further outwards to the very
tips of his physical body ; the feeling is similar to that
of pressing one's hand deep into a glove, only instead
of five fingers there are thousands. It is a strange land
to human consciousness, a land wherein the woods are
cities with the people living closely together, the
spinneys and coverts are outlying villages, and, in some
way, the whole is seen to be united, to be part of one
great consciousness, the great tree-being, whose children
all trees are.

The " tree-man " is the summation of the astral
consciousness of the tree, and he uses the etheric
double of the tree as a vehicle, through which he
receives physical sensation. Looked at from the point

of view of the group-soul, every tree within it is seen as an individual incarnation, varying in development chiefly according to age. The use of the word " being " must be accepted relatively, though the closer I get the more I realise that there is a definite entityship in the case of the large old trees, and that there is something which corresponds to family feeling at their level, a consciousness of group relationship. The strongest feeling of which they are capable results from the vivid play of the life force through the etheric double of the tree ; this is an ever-present and gradually increasing source of a sensation, which must be translated as one of pleasure.

Every tree has a vital heart, a sort of spleen and solar plexus in one, into which the life forces pour, and from which they are distributed throughout the whole system. As I sit leaning against a powerful and large beech tree, and am to some small measure in touch with the consciousness within, the continual thrill of this process is very noticeable—in fact, my whole body is vibrating to it, and the etheric and astral bodies are also powerfully affected ; it is a rippling, rhythmic sensation, with something faintly corresponding to a regular pulse at its source ; I can hear the sound of it, astrally, as if the tree were a tuning fork in continual vibration ; it gives me the impression of a singing note, a full-toned hum, coming from the very centre of the trunk and sounding throughout the whole system. When a gust of wind catches the tree, modulations occur ; they change and vary continually according to the strength and direction of the wind. The breeze is now very light and intermittent, and the change is not more than a quarter tone above and below the keynote.

This experience is awakening strange feelings, nay " memories " in me, as if it carried me back to remote periods when I lived in similar conditions ; indeed, it is all strangely familiar and grows more so, and, as I become more accustomed to the vibrations and more easily able to unify myself with them, I almost feel that the trees, in their turn, are aware in some dim fashion of those who love and admire them.

The new point of view which emerges from this experience, is that trees are not just growing wood, useful members of the vegetable kingdom, features of the landscape—they are living things and exceedingly sensitive. They are approaching the summit of their evolutionary mountain, nearing the limits of their kingdom.

The woods which clothe this valley have become full of living friends, and I seem to hear the murmur of their many voices as neighbour speaks to neighbour amid the primeval freshness and the clean, strong purity of the tree world.

I am conscious of a deep happiness and contentment, and the thought occurs to me that humanity might well endeavour to build into its character more of the rugged strength and stability, the deep rhythmic equipoise which characterise so many of the trees.

THE SPIRIT OF THE EARTH

NOTE BY A DEVA

August 23rd, 1925.

" All those things that you call ' Nature '—tree, flower, corn, root, grass, mountain, fell, hill and dale— are expressions of the life of the Great One, who has this earth as a physical body. You may think of rock as the skeleton and soil as the flesh, rivers as the blood vessels, the water of the rivers and the seas as the blood and the magnetic currents as flowing along the nerves of his body—the vegetation bearing the same relation to that body as hair does to yours.

You are right in supposing that the kingdom of Pan is included within it, though you have still much to learn of its place therein. Pan manifested, is an uprush of earth consciousness, a relatively active expression of that which is normally quiescent.

The Spirit of the Earth expresses itself through the earth as a form or vehicle, but not, as we of the human and deva kingdoms do, by its movement and activity so much, as through the growth and development of its natural products. In saying this, we must not forget that the revolution of the earth on its axis and its journey in its orbit round the sun constitute a form of movement, which also bears its part in the expression and evolution of the consciousness of the Spirit of the Earth, as if you expressed yourself by the growth and movement of your body alone. This mighty consciousness is spread equally throughout the whole globe, and has its centre or heart in the middle of the earth, and subsidiary centres at other parts, in relationship with particular areas on the surface. It is in these areas or force centres of the Spirit of the Earth that the great civilisations gather. Egypt, for example, is one, Shamballa is another, there is another in India, one in central Europe, one in Ireland—others where there are seas now, to be used by the humanities of the future. The hierarchies are aware of these centres and make use of them for the furtherance of their work. The Spirit of the Earth is an evolving being, as the globe is an evolving form, which has passed through all degrees of density, and, having reached the deepest point, has started its upward journey. The changes in the vegetation, the gigantic growths of the primeval forests, the developments of new species—of tree, cereal, fruit and flower—all these are the expressions of the evolving consciousness of the Spirit of the Earth. It sums up into a unity that portion of the One Life that is behind all manifested form on this earth, and in that sense it is a representative of the Logos. That stretching out of the tree consciousness, which you sensed the other evening, results from the upward pressure of its evolving life, just as do the volcano and the flood. From another point of view it is the lens, focussing the life of the Logos, and expressing it as the ceaseless and resistless urge, the driving power, which, being behind all form, produces growth, and without which there would be stagnation. The expression of its consciousness, however, is not limited to the vegetable and mineral kingdoms; it has produced other forms, neither human nor animal, it is true, but partaking of the appearance of both : these are the creatures of Pan. Strange and weird though they appear to you, they are natural expressions of certain aspects of its consciousness ; you might almost regard them as its play, or perhaps as being the result of certain experiments which it has made.

In the remote ages of the past, before the development of mind, these creatures of Pan were more objective, more material, did indeed roam the earth, and were occasionally contacted by primitive Arcadian man. As the great changes began to occur, which the development of emotion and mind wrought in human life, Pan was no longer a desirable associate, and was therefore withdrawn from the material plane, but he still exists and may still be found, as you have proved. The time may yet come in later days when the association will be resumed. Pan was on the downward arc when his cycle and that of humanity touched one another in the past : in the far future, when the corresponding point is reached in the next cycle, Pan will be on the path of return.

Amongst the many great changes that are occurring, one will arise as the result of what might be described as a stirring of the Spirit of the Earth within its form, a stirring which will bring certain aspects of its life nearer to the surface and more nearly within the reach of human consciousness. The effects of this will be many. One will be to draw men nearer to Nature, and so to keep them simple amid the ever-increasing complexity which is such a strongly marked characteristic of the present phase of human development. Contact with it will tend to develop the mystic side of human consciousness, and it will exercise a co-ordinating, synthesising and unifying influence upon man. All these developments, though apparently the results of many streams of life, are timed to take place at certain particular periods ; for, behind the diversity, behind even the Spirit of the Earth, there is the One Will which is omnipotent, the One Mind which is omniscient and the One Life which is omnipresent, and, co-ordinated by this, evolution proceeds irresistibly, perfectly, and in an ordered procession of events, on its majestic way."

The deva who gave this information commenced a regular system of teaching in 1926, the first results of which are being published under the title which he gave " The Brotherhood of Angels and of Men."

CHAPTER VIII

EXAMPLES OF CO-OPERATION BETWEEN DEVAS AND MEN

At the Shrine of St. Alban, in St. Albans Abbey.
November 9th, 1925.

THE only portion of the shrine which remains is the pediment, a beautiful and highly-decorated stone structure, which was rebuilt from the two thousand different fragments into which the original had been broken; they were discovered in the east wall of the Abbey, into which they had been built. In the base of the pediment, there are three diamond-shaped holes, called healing holes, two on the south side and one on the north, into which diseased limbs could be placed; tradition bears witness to the wonderful healing properties of the shrine.

The casket, which contained the actual relics and rested on the pediment, has been lost, together with its sacred contents. The shrine is now enclosed and protected by an iron railing.

One did not need to be very sensitive to realise that in spite of the absence of the relics, the shrine is very powerfully charged with their vibrations; its magnetism is of an order, which could be distinctly felt at etheric and even dense physical levels. Even the railings themselves are magnetised, as I soon discovered when leaning upon them to examine the shrine.

Clairvoyant investigation revealed the presence of a guardian deva, of considerable spiritual stature, great beauty, and of benevolent character. He recognised our party as devotees of St. Alban, and, as will be described later, he assisted us in the study of His Shrine.

The thought occurred to me, that it must be very limiting for such a deva to maintain, through the centuries, the guardianship even of such an important spiritual centre, and quickly the realisation came, that while he maintained a watchful care over the shrine, and one of his lower vehicles was permanently stationed there, his consciousness was quite free on the higher planes. He was assisted in his work, by a number of devas at lower stages of development than himself, who were largely responsible for the magnetic insulation of the sphere of influence, of which the shrine was the centre. The range of this was probably some twelve to fifteen feet in all directions, and the deva workers were seen passing round its outer edge, maintaining the circuit which was continually being broken by the passage of sightseers.

During the time of our stay in the shrine room, one of these devas appeared to be stationed at the doorway, which had an etheric and astro-mental door, and which it was his business to " close " ; he reminded me of the tyler of a masonic lodge. I saw at least one other of his brethren, who remained on the east side of the sphere, around which people were most frequently passing.

Every atom of the stone, brick and iron of the shrine itself was seen to be highly charged with a magnetism, which would be quite strong enough, in my opinion, to heal the sick under certain conditions. In the healing holes, this etheric force was strongly concentrated; each of the four inside surfaces of their diamond shape radiated power towards the centre, where the four streams appeared to meet; each of the holes, therefore, had become a highly-charged area.

At the astro-mental level the radiations of power from the shrine appeared to flow outwards evenly, in all directions, to the edge of the field of influence to which I have already referred; there was a continuous supply from some hidden source from which this steady and continuous outrush was maintained; it originated with the physical relics themselves in olden days, and the presiding deva told us that the Saint spent a part of His heaven life, following the St. Alban incarnation, in making and maintaining the links between Himself and the shrine, ensuring a continuance of the supply of power and in obtaining the co-operation of the devic hierarchy along the lines already described; that at later periods in His evolution He had consciously renewed the last two, and that now, as a living Adept,* He maintained a *rapport* with the shrine on the inner planes; the deva added that there was a probability of the Abbey being used as a spiritual centre in the future, and that it was for this reason, in addition to their value through the centuries, that such occult arrangements had been made.

I asked him if it would be permissible and possible for us to make physical links with the shrine, its power and himself, for the purposes of the different aspects

He who was St. Alban was, in a later incarnation, Francis Bacon; and, having reached Adeptship, is known as the Master Rakoczi, the Hungarian Adept of the ": Occult World."

of theosophical work, in which the four members of
the party were engaged, and particularly for healing.
His answer was a ready affirmative, and he graciously
suggested the means, which we eventually employed.
One member of the party, a mother of three children,
an earnest theosophical student and the secretary of a
Theosophical Society centre, used her wedding ring
for the purposes of an initial experiment.   After
demagnetisation, this was placed upon the shrine and
the deva immediately turned his attention upon it.
He seemed to have her children in his mind, when he
concentrated the healing forces of the shrine upon
the ring, which gradually became very highly charged
with a similar power ; as in the case of the other
objects which were magnetised later, every atom,
which entered into the composition of the ring, seemed
to be charged and the resultant force to be driven
downwards through the subplanes of the physical plane
until the whole etheric double of the ring, as well as its
physical molecules, were vibrating at the required
rate.   After a space of two or three minutes the ring
was literally glowing and had its own aura or sphere of
influence, which was very similar to that of the shrine
itself ; it seemed to me, that in the possession of this
ring, its owner now has a healing talisman, which she
will find to be of great assistance in her family responsi-
bilities.

I then asked her if there was any particular quality
which she wished to develop, and she suggested love
and compassion ; the deva consenting, we placed upon
the shrine her large gold theosophical seal.   The deva
concentrated his attention upon it, and gradually in
the astro-mental double of the seal, there appeared a

small heart-shaped centre of love force, a glowing rosy heart, built round and into the lines of force generated by the Egyptian *tau*, which appears in the middle of the symbol. When this was completely established, a soft green sphere was formed round it, representing the qualities of deep sympathy and compassion. The effect of this beautiful talisman will be gradually to build into the lady's aura and character the qualities with which it is impregnated, as well as to provide a link through which the power of the shrine, its deva and patron Saint, may be contacted at any time.

Another member of the party possessed a beautiful old Spanish cross of silver set with small diamonds; this had already been charged, to some extent, with the power of the great Master Rakoczi, who in a previous incarnation was St. Alban. The deva recognised this at once, and agreed with a radiant smile, to a further magnetisation. In this case, no special qualities were asked for, and he made the cross glow with the white fire of Atma, saying to its owner, " I give you the fire of the spiritual will to aid you on the path." Looking at her closely, he asked whether the Abbey and its surroundings seemed familiar to her, and seemed to suggest that he recognised her as a reincarnation of a former inhabitant of the district. This lady afterwards admitted that during the whole of the visit to St. Albans—the first in this life—she felt a curious sensation of having been there before. After the magnetisation of a silver symbol of the five-pointed star set in a circle of blue enamel, to serve as a personal link with the shrine and the deva, we endeavoured to express our gratitude for the blessings we had received by meditating together round the shrine upon the great Masters of the Theosophical Society; we tried to serve as channels for their benediction upon the Abbey, the shrine and its shining guardians. The deva acknowledged this with his radiant smile and, at parting, used the ancient formula, which showed his connection with the Mysteries and with the Great White Brotherhood, "May you soon reach the further shore."

In addition to the devas of the shrine, there was a great angel, who was in charge of the Abbey as a whole, and who presided over its activities as a centre of the Christian faith. He, too, was assisted by a number of his younger brethren, with the result that one felt that the Abbey of St. Albans was indeed a strong centre of spiritual power, and that from it there radiated upon the town an influence of spiritual peace and benediction.

OUR BLESSED LADY AND HUMAN MOTHERHOOD

In the course of some studies of the prenatal processes of incarnation, recently undertaken, I have been much struck by the important part which the devas play in the building of the subtle and physical bodies.

The particular case, which I was observing at short intervals, from the fourth to the ninth month, may have been a little unusual, as it seemed to me that the returning ego was particularly advanced, and might have special assistance, while, in addition, both parents are firmly established in thesophical knowledge and faith. I am inclined, none the less, to believe that much of what I shall attempt to describe is general in its application. When, with further study, our knowledge of the subject increases, it is hoped that a fairly detailed account of the processes involved may be issued in book form.

The whole of the complicated processes of taking on bodies of mental, astral, etheric and physical matter, in the case examined, appeared to be taking place under the supervision of a deva at the Causal or Arupa level ; under him were his mental and astral subordinates, while at the etheric and solid physical stages, the work of building the body was partly carried out by nature-spirits, under the control of the astral deva.

The function of the astral deva seems to be largely protective and supervisory : he receives information from the arupa deva of the result to be aimed at and of as much of the Karmic situation as it is necessary for him to know, and the matter is then built into the astral body, under his care. His brother at the mental level is in a precisely similar position.

Repeatedly, during the different observations, the extreme care, concentration and sense of responsibility, with which the devas do their work, became apparent. The astral deva, for example, frequently enfolded the astral and physical bodies of the embryo within himself, shielding them from harmful vibrations and warding off inharmonious influences.

In addition, he continually tried to share his own vivid devic life with the child, playing upon the subtler bodies with his personal force and brooding perpetually over them.

While watching him at work and trying to share in his consciousness, during the ninth month, it seemed as if he actually reverenced the growing bodies, so great was the care and tenderness with which his work was carried out ; it was on this occasion that a new pheno-

menon attracted my attention. I saw that the aura of
the deva had changed during the last month ; it was
so formed as to appear like a beautiful mantle of blue,
thrown over the head and shoulders, with one corner
also covering mother and child ; at this time the aura
of the child was largely enclosed within that of the
deva and looked like a large shimmering white egg, of
about four feet in height, shining through the auras of
deva and mother.

The blue mantle shone much more brightly, with a
silvery sheen, and, as the head of the deva was bent
down over his charges and his arms embraced them,
the effect was irresistibly reminiscent of Madonna and
child.

There was such a deep tenderness, such a truly
maternal spirit of love and joy and protection, that I
was profoundly touched by the vision ; seeking to
understand it more deeply and to trace the source of
this newly-introduced colour and form, I found my
consciousness being raised to the causal level, by some
power which drew and upheld me at those unaccustomed heights, and there I saw One so lovely, so truly
embodying the spirit of Motherhood, as of Womanhood,
that I knew Her as none other than the Blessed Mother
Herself.

Radiant, and beautiful is She beyond description.
She shines with all the glory of divinity, yet Her
" form " is that of a fresh young girl ; through the
wondrous eyes, there shines forth a glowing happiness,
an almost ecstatic bliss, which, in spite of its exaltation
and superhuman intensity, is full of the happy laughter
of children, strangely combined with the deep contentment of human maturity.

From this level, I realised that the devas previously seen were Her representatives and that as the time of birth drew near, so did she approach more closely, through Her messengers, to mother and child.

This closer touch gradually changed the appearance of the astral deva, who took on Her likeliness so closely, that he became in truth the angel of Her presence. I remembered the statement that, just as Our Lord is present on every occasion when the Holy Eucharist is performed through the Angel of the Presence, so is the Lady Mary present at the bedside of every mother at the sacrament of childbirth.

So close does She come, that She actually seems to share the pangs of birth, as well as the joys of parenthood ; indeed, I believe that She deliberately unifies Herself with the womanhood of the world, suffering with them all their pain, even their shame and degradation, in order that She may more truly share with them Her own divine achievement, Her wondrous power, Her all-embracing Love.

So I think does She experience with them all the joys of the first love, the fresh beauty of awakening womanhood, as well as the deep happiness of maturity, the joys of the wife and mother.

All these She sums up in Herself to perfection, and, out of the abundance of Her power and knowledge, She pours Herself out continually upon the womanhood of the world.

Her influence must increase the power, depth and beauty of the love of the maid for her man, give courage and endurance to the wife in the hours of her pain and trial and increase enormously the value to the ego of those expansions of consciousness, those deep changes of soul, which come to every woman, in some degree, when she passes into the valley of the shadow of death that a child may be born.

She seeks the perfection of the individual as of the race, and She works for it, through woman, seeking to exalt marriage and maternity, to restore to man the lost ideals of the deeply sacred nature of marriage and parenthood. She knows that thus a purer race will be born, a race that shall provide bodies ever more and more fit to be the temple of the indwelling God.

In this wonderful and beneficent atmosphere on the inner planes are the processes of incarnation carried out ; it is, I feel, for us to see to it that we provide conditions in the physical world that shall be worthy of the sacrificial blessing so freely and marvellously outpoured by Our Lady, the Queen of Angels, the " Mother " of the World.

CHRISTMAS AT HUIZEN, 1925

To have the privilege of being in or near the great European centre, of being received at the Master's House—De Duinen—of participating in the services of the little church of St. Michael and All Angels, is to be drawn very near to the heart of reality.

Dull indeed would be the senses of him who could not respond to the power, the wonder, and the joy and beauty, with which the whole place is literally saturated.

Strongest of all perhaps is the sense of power ; it can be felt, as one approaches, at a distance of quite half a mile from the estate ; at the heart of it there is perfect peace, complete tranquillity, but it manifests

itself outwardly as a great vortex of energy, the effect
of which may be very disturbing, until one finds what
I can only describe as the gyroscopic stability at the
heart.   There one finds a poised immobility, a calm
which no external agency could disturb.

The sense of wonder is produced by many factors;
to one belonging to the workaday business world, there
comes an increasing feeling of amazement, to find a
great fundamental and spiritual verity definitely and
clearly made manifest in this illusory world, which
habit has taught us to regard as concrete existence.
Here we find freedom from all personal trammels, utter
selflessness, completely impersonal dedication, without
any of those thoughts of self, of reward, of ambition,
however spiritual, which so often mar the offerings men
make to God.   One feels at Huizen, that there are no
enclosing boundaries, no self-limiting separations from
the outer world ; as if, in the heart of a great and popu-
lous city, there existed a beautiful private garden, continually made fair by lovely flowers, with smooth and
well-kept lawns, and many a shady arbour without any
fence to guard it, or any notice board bidding trespassers
beware ; on the contrary, the spirit of the fair garden of
the Masters at Huizen is one which welcomes the whole
world to the enjoyment of its beauties and its peace.

The angels visit Huizen.   They come not only for
the purpose of work in connection with the centre, but
that they too may be refreshed and uplifted, as are their
human brethren.   There seems to be a system of training for newly individualised angels brought by their
elders to be bathed in the powerful magnetism, to learn
their work and to find the Path.

In my experience of the kingdom of the shining

ones,—as yet but small—I have never encountered so much friendliness and readiness to co-operate.

Many are engaged in work of defence. A great centre like Huizen is not created and maintained without opposition. There is opposition from the ordinary world, in which unfortunately there is still to be found so much of bigotry, intolerance, hatred and ridicule of anything which either runs counter to man's prejudices or is beyond their understanding. There is opposition also from those sections of the Christian community, who, denying the all-embracing love of their Founder, frown upon a " new " religious movement, which would include all other faiths in one great brotherhood, which would give freely to all men such knowledge of the mysteries of God as they were capable of receiving, which would lift men from the darkness of that spiritual ignorance, in which it would almost seem they had been intentionally kept. Not only from these does opposition come, but also from those who have deliberately chosen the way of separateness, as their pathway to God.

During my short stay, I felt, on more than one occasion, that definite attempts were being made to find a place of entrance, to discover a weakness, a loop-hole which was not guarded, a joint in the armour that guards the unity of the brethren working here, through which an attack could be made.

Great as the privilege of living here undoubtedly is, great also is the responsibility, for unless perfect harmony, perfect understanding, complete mutual tolerance and an abiding sense of unity in a great work can be maintained, the weaknesses of humanity will manifest themselves and through them the attack will be made. It is not pleasant to contemplate the *Karma* of the person or group, which " let in " the forces of disruption. As far as one can judge at present, there seems to be no danger of such a catastrophe, and the devas work with such perfect unity, such absolute accord, that their guardianship, and the happy affection and mutual respect of their human co-workers, provide an impenetrable defence. The contemplation of these things produces the sense of wonder.

During the Christmas celebrations the sense of joy seemed to me the prevailing note ; it shone in the faces of priest, server, and congregation alike ; it pervaded the whole atmosphere of the festive season. Never before has the meaning of the Feast of Christmas seemed so clear and its message so real to me, as if the angels sang continually to us, " Lift up your hearts with joy, for Christ is truly born among men—verily He is with you now."

Consciousness of the indwelling Christ seemed to be awakened, as if He had at last come to dwell within the heart, and under the glowing radiance of His life, the petals of the mystic rose had begun to open to reveal some measure of His beauty.

In this atmosphere of inward communion and of joy, Christmas passed ; on December 28th * a new light seemed to shine upon us, bringing to us a growing feeling of His physical and human nearness, as if the literal meaning of the Feast of Christmas were being understood, and the Presence on a thousand altars had come to us, in another and more human way ; as the week

* Some weeks after this was first written the news came that the Lord had spoken once more at the great jubilee gathering of the Theosophical Society at Adyar on December 28th, 1925.

progressed this feeling deepened, and the message of the Star was combined with that of the Church ; some of us felt that a holy gladness had run over the face of the earth, because the Lord Who had so graciously taken up His dwelling in our hearts, had also come to us in an external and objective visitation.

Thus indeed Christmas has been for us a time of joy.

Wherever there are angels, there is beauty. Huizen, being an angel centre, is therefore a place where beauty is always manifest. Angels seem to welcome all who enter the gates ; sometimes they greet their fellow worshippers on their way to the church and, last night, after solemn benediction, as the dusk of the last evening of the old year was falling, it seemed to me that two angels moved one on either side of us as we walked home. Their auras met in front of us and behind us, and, in the charmed atmosphere of their protecting friendship, we felt that truly the time was drawing near when, once more, angels should walk with men.

Many were seen returning through the air towards the church : perhaps on this, the last might of the passing year, they thus accompanied to their homes all those who had joined with them in worship and praise.

During the services, always so beautiful, the angels seem to join with the people and to share their happiness, holding a joint service on the higher planes. Glorious indeed were the glimpses, which I occasionally caught of their outpouring of devotion and love, as, in great companies, they " sang " with us, till the whole of the Eastern temple, which the Holy Eucharist builds, was filled with the music of these heavenly choirs. Beyond the range of my limited vision, I sensed other more glorious and majestic " shining ones," performing, at their level, their part in building the centre in the inner worlds.

Strange though it may sound, some of this inner beauty and holiness is beginning to shine through all those who are so zealously working here ; at times I almost caught my breath, to see a form transfigured, a face lit up with a glow of saintliness, as if a wondrous transformation were taking place in the hearts and minds, as also in the very atoms of the bodies of those who, in this place, regularly come to serve their Lord. They are themselves growing like the angels, not only in their appearance, but in the unanimity of their conscious participation in the inner work of the sacraments. Steeped, as they are, in the knowledge of the science of the Church, the effect produced is extremely rapid and sure, and the temple, not built with hands, is erected with perfect precision and with a minimum of effort. The result of all this is that, in the little church there is an atmosphere, which is only approached by some of the very old cathedrals of Europe, and from it there radiates, far and wide, a power and a blessing which is hardly equalled in range by the greatest and oldest of the churches of the West. In the heart of all this beauty there is Love, that Divine and Perfect Love which casts out all fear and radiates from Him, Who is the Heart of the World.

At Huizen one feels so near to Him, as to be indeed " lifted up into the immensity of His Love." And so, in Huizen, the New Year's resolution is born, to try so to live that His love may shine forth through us, with undiminished glory, unsullied by any thought of self, undimmed by the shadow of aught that is unclean, that so illumined we may indeed " breathe forth the fragrance of a Holy Life." From the depths of our hearts do we thank those Great Ones, Who have given Huizen to the world, for from it there flows an influence which, if we can but use it, will change this sorrowful world of ours into an " everglowing star of love."

Let me close this all too inadequate description with the collect of St. Michael and All Angels :—

" Almighty and everlasting God, with all our hearts we praise Thee, for the great glory of Thy Most Holy Angels ; we thank Thee, for the great glory of Thy Most Holy Angels ; we thank Thee for Their wonderful wisdom, Their supreme strength, Their radiant beauty ; and as Their resistless power is used always and utterly in Thy service, so may we, following zealously Their resplendent example, devote ourselves wholly to the helping of our brethren, through Christ our Lord." Amen.

DR. BESANT AT THE QUEEN'S HALL, 1925

ONE imagines that the Queen's Hall in London must be an ideal place, for the special work which Dr. Besant carries out within its walls.

The fact that it has been used continuously for many years for concerts at which only the best music is performed is in itself sufficient to have generated an atmosphere of harmony and beauty, and to have established a lofty rate of vibration in its mental and astral surroundings. Further, if we remember that every physical atom of its walls and furnishings has been impressed, year after year, with the utmost regularity, with the vibration of this music, we shall realise that the whole place, and all within it, is very highly charged ; in addition, the President has used it repeatedly for her great series of lectures, filling it with her powerful magnetism, and with the mighty force of the Masters, Whose representative she is.

The nickel-plated rod on which she rests her hands must be magnetised for all time, so that everyone who stands behind it, whether to speak, sing or conduct, must be beneficially affected.

About a quarter of an hour before the lecture begins, the atmosphere of the hall suddenly becomes electric ; one is conscious of a change and a certain tension in the psychic conditions ; it feels rather like a room, which has been subjected to powerful and continuous ionisation. At first I attributed this to the general feeling of expectancy and to the rapid filling of the hall, but an endeavour to trace it further, led me to the conclusion that it is due to two causes. One is that a powerful and concentrated attention is turned upon the meeting by the Great Ones, Who, knowing that a member and representative of the Brotherhood is about to use it for furthering the work, upon which They are all engaged, turn their attention upon the scene of her labours and by this means create an atmosphere, in the inner worlds, in which the best results may be achieved.

The other cause is the arrival and activity of certain devas, who appear about this time, and take up their stations, some high in the air above the hall and others at different places within it.

As the lecture proceeds the whole hall gradually becomes enveloped in a blazing globe of light ; from its outside, this looks like a huge iridescent bubble, which eventually fills with light and colour and takes on the appearance of a luminous solid sphere. From the centre a continual stream of opalescent light is pouring in all directions, a fountain of power, which wells up continually within the sphere. It actually hums like a great engine, generating an apparently inexhaustible stream of force, which shoots out to the circumference of the sphere, filling it with an infinite number of fine lines, so that if one took a section through it, it would look like a great wheel, solid from hub to rim, because the spokes were set so close together.

The power seems to leap forth, sweeping all other influences before it, and completely magnetising everything in its path.

An opalescent colour effect is produced in which every colour of the spectrum flashes and gleams in delicate shades, as the force rushes forth. The whole audience is close enwrapped in this globe of light, and each aura and every consciousness, is illumined by the contact.

This radiant power gradually increases its range as the lecture proceeds, first embracing the front rows of the orchestra and stalls, and then quickly reaching the outer walls of the hall. This takes about twenty minutes, when a consolidation appears to take place and the sphere, at first unevenly filled with light and colour, begins to become solid.

This process is resisted here and there by individuals scattered about the hall; for though it might appear that the whole audience is gradually brought into agreement with the main theme of the speaker, such is in fact far from being the case.

Some—feeling conscious both of a power, which includes them in its radiation and seems to sway the intellect, and of a sympathy and understanding, which draw them even against their will—endeavour to protect themselves from such influence. At first the force flows *round* these people, then, after the sphere is marked out and begins to be filled, it starts to beat against their auras, gradually raising their tone—though, of course, much more slowly than in the case of those who more readily respond.

Every member of the audience is blessed and uplifted as a result of his presence at the lecture. The effect, of course, varies, but those who are willing and able to respond, whose hearts are already filled with love and veneration for the white-haired figure from whom all this mighty power comes forth, are, literally, illuminated throughout their whole nature. Sluggish auras gradually awaken, crusts of habit and shells of prejudice begin to break down, until, finally, in very many cases, the whole being is vibrating in tune with the outrushing force, the aura being toned up until it glows with a reflection of the light which shines from her presence.

In addition to this, each of the twelve people who sit on either side of their leader upon the platform, is making his own particular contribution to the work which is being done. This appears, from one point of view, as a stream of colour flowing outwards from each one, a deep rich sapphire blue, for example, is seen shooting through the sphere—a royal red, a soft sky blue, a fine yellow—as each figure shines with the colour of his own temperament and ray.

The difference of ray shows in other ways too ; for those whose nature it is to work along scientific lines add to the general stream by projecting, into different parts of the hall, and towards particular people, specially directed currents of force.

From the head of the speaker wave upon wave of golden yellow light emanates, and through which lances and spears of more intense light continually flash. These are followed by the physical expression of an idea.

Another result of the lecture, upon the inner planes, is the gradual construction of a symmetrical mento-astral form—the thought form of the speech as a whole ; it looks to me rather like a squarely built castle, rising storey upon storey, from the solid foundation, upon which her speeches are always built ; its white walls are bathed in a colour like the glowing golden sunlight of some tropical land. This form rises gradually from the level of her shoulders, mounting slowly upwards as she proceeds, until the flat top or roof reaches high up above the ceiling of the hall, out into the upper air ; it is remarkably clear cut, and its castle-like appearance is increased by the presence of a number of oblong windows, all showing different colours, as if a lamp within projected the various colours of the spectrum. Each of these windows corresponds to an idea, a set of facts, or an illustration used during the progress of the lecture.

When the address is finished, the connection between this thought form and its creator breaks, and it rises upwards, high into the heavens, and there floats, an image of glowing beauty, a reservoir of power, a treasure house of ideas.

The invisible audience is far more numerous than the visible ; crowds of discarnate men and women hover around the great hall listening to the speech and bathing in the stimulating magnetism, drawn thither by the display of power and light, the glow of which is visible for miles around in the astral world and attracts its inhabitants to the scene.

Other helpers, too, stand near the speaker, stately and majestic figures, making use of the occasion of such a large gathering, and the strength available from the concentration of such a large number of followers and fellow workers.

As previously mentioned, the deva hierarchy is represented in full measure, members of this race assisting in the work ; some, ranged round the outside edges of the sphere, stand like angel sentinels against the walls behind the three levels of seats ; they conserve the power ; and some of them, after the form is firmly established, turn their attention upon the people, both visible and invisible, and begin to work definitely upon and through them.

As I am specially interested in and attracted towards the devas, I found myself responding very readily to their endeavours. Their touch is always a source of joy to me, as is the radiant beauty of their smile of recognition and acknowledgment.

At the beginning of the lecture, I thought I saw a deva at each door of the gallery in which I sat, and earlier, while I was acting as steward, it seemed to me that they exerted force upon every person who entered, sometimes touching them directly, and sometimes using the stewards as channels to the same end.

With all this splendour in the invisible world, one might think that the limit of beauty and power had been already reached, but as each great truth was driven home, as each beautiful ideal was presented, as some special appeal was made—the golden voice still deepening and strengthening with the intense earnestness of the teacher—an additional flow of power flashed forth ; literally blinding flames of light blaze up at these moments, when the world's greatest orator puts forth the full power of that art of which she is so supremely master.

As the winged minutes pass, every ear entranced by the magic of that voice of surpassing beauty, the brilliance of the sphere of light increases, until its radiance almost blinds the inner eye, nor does its splendour diminish until, at last, the lecture is finished and we see the white-robed figure turning, as she leaves the platform, to bow her acknowledgment of the applause with which the address is received.

*   *   *   *   *

We are not denied the joys of helping in all this.

There are many ways in which we can co-operate.

There is much work to be done beforehand, and at the time itself, and many stewards are needed in so large a hall. Those who are not claimed by this physical office can help spiritually, by arriving well before the lecture begins and meditating with all their strength upon the subject of the address, endeavouring to realise its deepest spiritual aspects and to bring them down to the level of the general understanding.

Those who know something of the work being done can, while the thought structure is in the building, steady the people nearest them, helping them to readjust themselves to their highly-charged surroundings, thus creating a receptive atmosphere, and shouldering a little—however little it may be—of our

beloved leader's burden. When the stillness and recep-
tivity are fully established, we may be used to focus
the outpoured strength, here and there about the hall,
or to channel the forces of the blessing which the Devas
and the Great Ones are showering upon the people
assembled and upon the surrounding neighbourhood.

"HARK THE HERALD ANGELS SING"

October, 1925.

Last night I had an experience which reminded me
very strongly of the visit of the Angels to the shepherds, to herald the birth of the Christ-child in
Bethlehem.

After retiring to our beds in the garden hut in which
we sleep, and as I lay looking out of the wide-open doors
at the stars, which lit a typical late October sky, I saw
a group of angels floating slowly across the heavens.
At first I took them to be thought-forms generated
from one or other of the churches in the neighbourhood,
and ensouled by nature-spirits, because they so closely
resembled the typical angel of mediæval religious art,
and of orthodox Christian angelology. In long full
flowing robes of shining white, they floated with a
poetic swinging motion, bearing such symbols in their
hands as madonna lilies, ears of corn, and, to me, unknown flowers of long and slender stems.

As I was watching them, there suddenly appeared,
framed in the doorway of the hut, a wonderful deva
messenger. His expression and vibration, and the
radiant outrushing forces of his brilliantly coloured aura
were distinctly non-human and bore very little resemblance to the conceptions presented with so much

beauty to us by the old masters; their angels resemble beautiful human beings, benevolent and serene, rather overdressed in the fashions of the day, and floating in graceful poses, as if suspended in the air. Very different indeed was the vivid and vital being who hovered just above the ground outside the door by which he was framed. He was distinctly of male type, and the face was virile and strong, the brow and eyes, particularly, were noble and commanding. The hair was swept back from the forehead and streamed out behind him in constant motion, like a halo of flickering fire.

He enfolded us in his aura, causing us to vibrate in harmony with him ; he seemed to give us the blessing of the devas, and then began to repeat the ancient message given to the shepherds of old, " Behold, I bring you glad tidings of great joy, which shall be to all people. For unto us a child is born, unto us a son is given ; and the government shall be upon his shoulder, and his name shall be called Wonderful, Counsellor, The Mighty God, The Everlasting Father, The Prince of Peace."

As he did this, there appeared behind him a number of other angels, approaching and descending in two long lines from the remote distance ; they were all surrounded and irradiated by a glowing brilliance of white and silvery blue ; many bore stringed or wind instruments, and many were singing, and all around them and in between their two ranks, were the winged heads of babies, singing in a soft yet silvery treble, which sounded octaves above the physical scale.
was like a heavenly choir of angels bringing the tiding of great joy to men, and as they approached our " bedroom," the lines opened and passed one on either

side of it, blessing and magnetising it and the ground on which it stood.

Slowly the long procession of radiant messengers passed through the garden, over the fields, down the hill, through the town that lies in the hollow and on into the distance, flooding the inner world with their light and with the great message of the Coming of the Saviour of men. I saw them gradually disappear over the distant hills ; their music died away, but the blessing of their presence remained. Perhaps it was an angel choir encircling the globe, as part of the work of preparing the hearts and minds of men for the coming of the Lord.

Once more our visitor blessed us, stretching forth his hands towards us and pouring forth his deva power. Then with a grave inclination of the head, he rose upwards and vanished from our sight.

*   *   *   *   *

His prophecy was fulfilled, for the Lord spoke to men once more on December 28th, 1925, and on July 27th, 1926.

Armistice Day, 1923

There are two impressions of November 11th, 1923, which will live long in the memory : one received in silence, the other in sound.

*   *   *   *   *

At the Cenotaph

Whitehall, under a bright November sun which shone from a clear blue sky. Crowds densely packed, and in the centre the white Cenotaph, its base covered with flowers. Royalty, uniforms and the people.

Eleven o'clock. Silence. Peace.

In the upper air is a far greater gathering of the tens of thousands of the dead. They assembled in a widening circle, rising from the centre, poised just above the heads of those who mourned; some were in uniform, some in mufti, others in flowing robes. In the hearts and on the faces of many there shone a joy, a real peace, and about them a great light.

Angels, too, there were in the throng, bathing the scene in the splendid and vivid colours of their auric robes. Soft greens, lavenders, brilliant shades of violet mingled with the golden light in which the whole scene was set, the light of that level where alone true unity is found.

Many of the departed saw the earthly ceremony, recognised their friends, and responded to their loving remembrance, loved them for their pain.

This impression was received from the heart of another, and even deeper, silence into which a few friends had fallen, as they gathered together at the same hour in order to dedicate themselves anew to their Lord and to unite with those who in Whitehall and throughout the land were silently remembering the dead.

We, too, felt a presence and caught a glimpse of the King in His beauty; we, too, felt that joy which touched the hearts of the dead and shone from their faces. For a moment the Christ consciousness seemed within our grasp, there was no separateness, we were one.

And the Voice said, " Behold, I am with you always, even unto the end of the world."

THE ALBERT HALL AND THE WORLD REQUIEM

A vast and white-robed chorus, spreading like two wings on either side of the large orchestra ; the great organ with its lights, and one man controlling with his baton, the whole, and from it calling forth wondrous potencies of sound.

Once more we were lifted up into Heaven, Devachan, the place of the angels, yes and even higher, for inspired genius brought near, very, very near again the vision of the Lord.

Colour, radiance, beauty, these are but feeble words with which to describe the state to which we were lifted, the glory that was ours.

Before the performers there appeared to stand the figure of an angel, through whose aura all the music passed ere it reached the ears of the audience. Massed in great numbers, angel children, their winged faces everywhere, were singing, for the whole of that beauty of sound was not physical. The physical sound awakened, evoked the Heavenly Chorus, and, under the genius of one man, the music of the spheres seemed to be sounding forth indescribably sweet and with an all-compelling beauty.

* * * * *

" Behold under the firmament are the Cherubim and Seraphim."

" And the noise of their wings is as the noise of great waters."

" And I hear the voice of angels round about the
   throne."

" And the number of them is ten thousand times ten
   thousand."

" And thousands of thousands."

" They are the angels of the Lord : His elect angels :
   stewards of the mysteries of God : His angels that
   do His commandments."

" And behold ! above the firmament is the likeness of
   a throne."

" A brightness as the colour of amber and as the
   appearance of a rainbow of fire."

" And a cloud of glory shineth round about within it."

" This is the appearance of the likeness of the glory of
   the Lord before Whom the Seraphim ever veil their
   faces."

" And behold out of the fiery cloud a voice saying,
   This is My beloved Son in Whom I am well pleased ;
   hear ye Him."

        " The World Requiem," by J. H. Foulds.

With such words and with heavenly music was the
great message given forth, with a perfection of beauty
that must surely have touched all hearts.

Vision followed upon vision, as uplifted by the music
some of its effects came within the reach of consciousness. Sometimes the vast dome of the deep blue sky
of night with white angels poised beneath the stars ;
then a still and sleeping earth, shrouded in a mystic
green, which blended with the blue, and again angels,
always angels, walking majestically upon earth ;
across the strange scene shimmering glories passed,
roseate dawns, bright noon days and gleaming sunsets,

wondrous beyond telling, each taking forms innumerable ; now with clear-cut outline, vast music forms filled the field of vision, now globes of shimmering radiance, which vanished in a myriad rainbow hues.

At one period a white cross was slowly built and floated higher and higher up into the vault of Heaven— the symbol of Life, formed by living sound. Later came the pentagram, the outline of a great five-pointed star, which flashed forth fully formed in lines of light.

And all the time we were enwrapped with tenderness and sweetness, in a beauty, a musical enchantment that blessed while it enchanted. Compassion and consolation came to us in colour and in sound. Hope filled our breasts during the immortal hour, with which John Foulds blessed our day of remembrance.

Blessed we were indeed, for even the angels sang for us, and it was a joy to think of our dead.

ANGELS AND MUSIC

An interesting incident connected with an angel friend occurred during a Kreisler recital on November 20th, 1922. During the later portion of the programme, the effect of which had been to raise my consciousness to a condition of exaltation, I became aware of the familiar vibrations of an angel friend. Exerting considerable pressure, he came very close, saying, " Listen intently, and I will listen through you." A change in consciousness occurred, in which I lost none of my physical awareness, but in which I knew that the visitor was using my body. As is so often the case, during close contact with the deva kingdom, the sense of hearing was stimulated very considerably, and I heard music as I had never heard it before, with a keenness of auditory perception, which, had it been ocular, would be termed microscopic. Each note, whether of piano or violin, seemed to be a separate life and was visualised mentally as globular, or ovoid, according to its time value. Within its centre was a core which was the soul of the note.

I was also conscious of some of the thoughts and feelings of the angel, which seemed to be to the effect that all music existed on its own plane of consciousness, was thought of, by him, in terms of colour, and as being externally manifested on its own plane in the form of mighty angels ; he regarded music as a kingdom of Nature, with its own inhabitants, which exists side by side with ours, and is an expression of the creative Word ; it appeared also that when the instruments were played, each note opened a valve or aperture, allowing corresponding music to pass through to the physical plane. The effect of this conception was most curious to watch. Every single note on both instruments was mentally visualised, as passing through the valve, which closed as the note died away. The interpreter seemed to stand with his head in the music kingdom and the idea came that all the great musicians are messengers from the Guardians of the kingdom of music to an evolving humanity, just as the great Rulers, Teachers and Healers of the world are messengers of the Great White Brotherhood.

In the case of Pachmann, it appeared as if a guardian angel stood behind him whilst he was playing. As he walked on to the platform, I received an immediate impression of a great ego, limited and confined in an

aged body. As he began to play, however, the real man
appeared gradually to stand upright, a wonderfully
powerful, dignified figure—youthful in appearance but
like him in feature. During and after the performance
of each piece, Pachmann was in a condition approaching childishness, in which his brilliant technique seemed
absurdly easy. On his face there was frequently a
smile, soft and child-like, yet the concentrated intent-
ness of the ego never wavered for an instant, and I saw
where the real power was being applied.

The guardian angel, who showed no particular sex
differentiation, was about ten feet in height, and remained motionless behind the performer, floating with
its feet some eighteen inches above the platform. In its
right hand it bore an instrument resembling a post-horn ;
the flow of its aura was so arranged as to produce an
effect of folded wings, the points of which reached
forward and downwards in a graceful sweep and
rested on the ground on either side of the musician.
The angel's left hand hung loosely at its side ; the pose
was majestic, the face young and beautiful, the whole
reminding me of Watts's picture " The Silent Watcher."
This figure remained on the platform during the performance of each of Chopin's works ; it became invisible
to me while the performer was not playing. They
formed a wonderful trio—these three—the simple
sweet-natured communicative genius of flawless technique and perfect ease of accomplishment, the intensely
concentrated egoic representation of him, and the
guardian angel, who protected him from all harm, and
provided the necessary atmosphere and inner seclusion
in which the genius could be inspired. Again, as is so
frequently observed in the case of deva workers, there

was a suggestion of a still Higher Consciousness, in contact with which the work was being done.

At the Kreisler concert I did glimpse one of the mighty Angels of music, but an attempt to find words for a description has failed so far. I must simply say that it was a Being, human in form, of inconceivable splendour and unimagined glory; it shone radiantly, and, in addition it " sounded " marvellously, as though its nature were expressed equally in sound as in light; it gave forth continuously one main resounding tone, with a multitude of over-tones. Some conception of this angel may perhaps be gained, if one tries to imagine a world of ineffable glory, in which lives a Being, manifesting by means of a yet greater glory; a world of Divine Sound, within which is an incarnated system of music, giving forth continually its own glorious contribution, the expression, in its own world, of its individual existence.

I think we may assume that the Gandharvas work side by side with the members of the human hierarchy at their own level, and like them, are in graded orders, which take their share in the activities of the Solar System as a whole, as well as in those of each planet. They are the divine Harmony incarnate; that Harmony finds its way through graded orders of beings to the dull ears of men, as music.

In music, therefore, do we not hear the voice of God, and does not the interpreter, whether individual, orchestra or choir, become for the time being the very mouthpiece of the Creator—an expression of the First Cause ?

The sincere and impersonal artist receives, according to his capacity, that touch from the God of his Art which may translate him into a genius. Should he prostitute his power, the magical touch awakens but his lower self and he falls a slave to his own desires. True genius means contact with the Monad, and it is the devas who can and do produce the temporary connection, long before it could be effected by the normal processes of evolution. This is true of every branch of art, but especially of music.

PURIFYING THE ATMOSPHERE OF A CITY

The Cotswolds. August 26th, 1926.

Before us a broad landscape stretches for thirty or forty miles to the distant mountains of Wales ; behind and above the mountains the sun is setting in a golden glow. The plains of the heavens are peopled with countless numbers of sylphs, flying like great human-bodied seagulls across the sky. An " army " of sylphs is concentrated above the city which is visible some eight or ten miles away, with its ancient cathedral tower standing out boldly above its smoky atmosphere. The astral aura of the city resembles a great bubble, as if blown from the ground ; it envelops the city, and rises about 1,000 feet into the air ; within it the astral atmosphere is dark, its colour deepening nearer to the ground ; heavy dull browns interspersed with streaks of lurid red and dark green, in some places in patches, floating loose, in others concentrated and fixed, are to be seen. All the higher and more lovely shades rise to the top, making a false sky, a kind of dome of blue, rose and apple-green.

From the cathedral a fountain of light and power pours up into the air ; light also shines from it upon its immediate neighbourhood. The sylphs are working at the lower stratum, level with the houses, which is dark throughout the streets. These radiant beings of light and beauty, pure whiteness and aerial vitality, are plunging through the bubble, down into that dark swamp of selfishness and vice. Their presence breaks it up, forces it to circulate, and then they bear its coarse matter in their auras, all sullied and befouled, up into the air, rising slowly as if with pain ; up, up they fly, then outwards, gradually expanding their auric wings, and dissipating the cloying, clogging mire. Watching one poised in mid-air, driving the dark mist away, I see him meditating : he passes into ecstasy, his face shining with joy through the shadow of the burden which he bears ; then he draws down power from above, it descends into head and sweeps throughout his being ; its electric, energising power is so great, that it revivifies his aura, so that the play of its forces is quickened and the streams of auric power gradually resume their vivid flow outwards from the centre, dispersing into space the astral evil which had been voluntarily absorbed.

By their hundreds they are working in this way, reminding me of miners going down into the pit, from which they emerge begrimed and darkened ; by this means the sylphs clean the astral atmosphere of the ancient city, literally washing its streets and houses : in certain areas where they have achieved a measure of success, they liberate and direct streams of energy into the dark places, like firemen turning on the hose.

Presiding over them as they work is the Genius of this great plain, an angel God in titanic human form. His presence and his power is impressed upon the whole region which he rules. He himself is visible at the mental level, his face impassive, godlike in its calm, majestic and utterly serene. Rulership and stability characterise him. Under his directions, his aerial subjects, the radiant and " silent-footed sylphs," labour. One vast army, as we have seen, works for men in village, town and city ; others for the vegetable world which beautifies the plain, while others yet are seen disporting themselves in angel aeronautics, wheeling, whirling and flashing across the sky.

ORDER FROM YOUR FAVORITE BOOKSELLER OR CALL FOR OUR FREE CATALOG

Of Heaven and Earth: Essays Presented at the First Sitchin Studies Day, edited by Zecharia Sitchin. ISBN 1-885395-17-5 • 164 pages • 5 1/2 x 8 1/2 • trade paper • illustrated • $14.95

God Games: What Do You Do Forever?, by Neil Freer. ISBN 1-885395-39-6 • 312 pages • 6 x 9 • trade paper • $19.95

Space Travelers and the Genesis of the Human Form: Evidence of Intelligent Contact in the Solar System, by Joan d'Arc. ISBN 1-58509-127-8 • 208 pages • 6 x 9 • trade paper • illustrated • $18.95

Humanity's Extraterrestrial Origins: ET Influences on Humankind's Biological and Cultural Evolution, by Dr. Arthur David Horn with Lynette Mallory-Horn. ISBN 3-931652-31-9 • 373 pages • 6 x 9 • trade paper • $17.00

Past Shock: The Origin of Religion and Its Impact on the Human Soul, by Jack Barranger. ISBN 1-885395-08-6 • 126 pages • 6 x 9 • trade paper • illustrated • $12.95

Flying Serpents and Dragons: The Story of Mankind's Reptilian Past, by R.A. Boulay. ISBN 1-885395-38-8 • 276 pages • 6 x 9 • trade paper • illustrated • $19.95

Triumph of the Human Spirit: The Greatest Achievements of the Human Soul and How Its Power Can Change Your Life, by Paul Tice. ISBN 1-885395-57-4 • 295 pages • 6 x 9 • trade paper • illustrated • $19.95

Mysteries Explored: The Search for Human Origins, UFOs, and Religious Beginnings, by Jack Barranger and Paul Tice. ISBN 1-58509-101-4 • 104 pages • 6 x 9 • trade paper • $12.95

Mushrooms and Mankind: The Impact of Mushrooms on Human Consciousness and Religion, by James Arthur. ISBN 1-58509-151-0 • 103 pages • 6 x 9 • trade paper • $12.95

Vril or Vital Magnetism, with an Introduction by Paul Tice. ISBN 1-58509-030-1 • 124 pages • 1/2 x 8 1/2 • trade paper • $12.95

The Odic Force: Letters on Od and Magnetism, by Karl von Reichenbach. ISBN 1-58509-001-3 • 192 pages • 6 x 9 • trade paper • $15.95

The New Revelation: The Coming of a New Spiritual Paradigm, by Arthur Conan Doyle. ISBN 1-58509-220-7 • 124 pages • 6 x 9 • trade paper • $12.95

The Astral World: Its Scenes, Dwellers, and Phenomena, by Swami Panchadasi. ISBN 1-58509-071-9 • 104 pages • 6 x 9 • trade paper • $11.95

Reason and Belief: The Impact of Scientific Discovery on Religious and Spiritual Faith, by Sir Oliver Lodge. ISBN 1-58509-226-6 • 180 pages • 6 x 9 • trade paper • $17.95

William Blake: A Biography, by Basil De Selincourt. ISBN 1-58509-225-8 • 384 pages • 6 x 9 • trade paper • $28.95

The Divine Pymander: And Other Writings of Hermes Trismegistus, translated by John D. Chambers. ISBN 1-58509-046-8 • 196 pages • 6 x 9 • trade paper • $16.95

Theosophy and The Secret Doctrine, by Harriet L. Henderson. Includes **H.P. Blavatsky: An Outline of Her Life,** by Herbert Whyte, ISBN 1-58509-075-1 • 132 pages • 6 x 9 • trade paper • $13.95

Printed in the USA
CPSIA information can be obtained
at www.ICGtesting.com
LVHW041147171023
761328LV00059B/845